CU00828246

QUICKSILVER

THE MERCURIAL EMIL ZÁTOPEK

Pat Butcher

Globerunner Productions

First published in Great Britain in 2016 by
Globerunner Productions

A CIP catalogue record for this book is
available from the British Library

ISBN 978-0957033221

Typset in Great Britain by Peter Nichols

Printed and bound in Great Britain by CPI Group (UK) Ltd, Croydon CR0 4YY

www.globerunner.org

Zane Branson, *In Memoriam*

ALSO BY PAT BUTCHER

The Perfect Distance
Ovett & Coe: The Record-Breaking Rivalry

The Destiny of Ali Mimoun

'Ensuite la légende s'en mêla et il devint,
même pour lui, difficile de faire la part
exacte entre le vrai, l'exagération et le mensonge'

Le Petit Saint, Georges Simenon

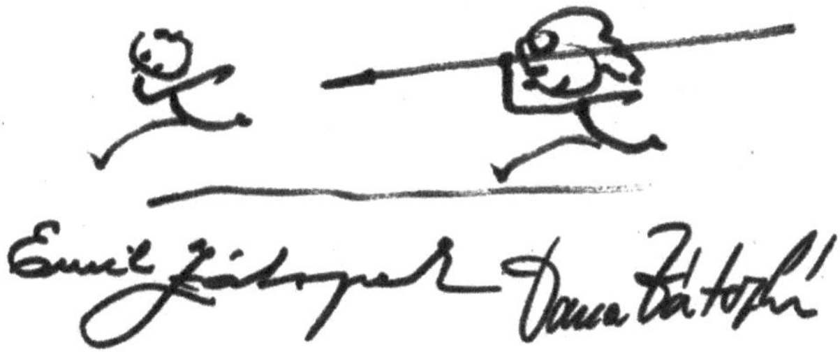
Emil Zátopek
Dana Zátopková

1.

An old man with ruddy features and gleaming eyes opened the door, beamed, and beckoned us in. He welcomed us in English, French and Czech, and led us through the narrow corridor, strewn with bikes, boxes and bottles, until we got to a bright, homely kitchen where his wife was preparing a pot of coffee to accompany the plate of open-sandwiches waiting on the table. She greeted us with equal warmth. Later, I would hear this welcome characterised as typical Wallachian hospitality, in the Moravian style chalet that the pair had built for themselves on the edge of this 'foreign' capital of Prague.

There was nothing on the walls and cabinets to indicate that this was one of the most successful couples in Olympic history – who had once won four gold medals between them in the same week, two inside half an hour. But, as I was to discover, neither of them had much time for trophies; they had given most of them away, including one of the best and brightest, an Olympic gold medal, in one of the most selfless acts of generosity and appreciation as it is possible to imagine.

While my interpreter exchanged pleasantries with his wife, the old man sidled up to my shoulder and quietly suggested, in a surprisingly thin voice, that I might want to forego the coffee, and dive straight into a bottle of Pilsner. It was 9.30am. Since I had long taken an oath of abstinence – until 8pm in the evening – as much as to offset the well-earned accusation of alcoholic indulgence which accompanies the journalist worldwide, as to preserve a degree of coherence, I demurred. I have still not forgotten this slight to our host, but I regret even more than I cannot boast that I once drank with Emil Zátopek.

2.

If I couldn't run like Emil Zátopek, the next best thing was to write a book about him. The former only ever had a slim chance of happening, and despite the moderately successful career of a county champion, the Olympic dream evaporated well before my 30th birthday. A decade later, I became an athletics journalist, at a time when the sport was burgeoning. The list of subjects during the 1980s and 1990s seemed endless – Sebastian Coe, Steve Ovett, John Walker, Steve Cram, Saïd Aouita, Haile Gebrselassie, Paul Tergat, Kenenisa Bekele, Carl Lewis, Ben Johnson, Ed Moses, Michael Johnson, Sergey Bubka, Mary Decker, Zola Budd, Flo-Jo, Heike Drechsler, Marita Koch, and dozens more; then there were the historical figures – Roger Bannister, Herb Elliott, Fanny Blankers-Koen, Michel Jazy, Gaston Roelants, Alain Mimoun, Gunder Hägg, Arne Andersson, Ron Clarke. I met and profiled them all during a 30 year career as an international journalist.

You'll note the pride of place given to middle-distance runners. That's not difficult to explain. I was a miler myself, albeit not a very good one. In any case, middle-distance running was the touchstone of international track and field athletics. And the men who epitomised that most for the era which transformed athletics from amateur to professional in the last two decades of the 20th century were Coe and Ovett. And that's why I eventually wrote a book about them.

But Zátopek was always nagging in the background. He'd been one of the inspirations for me starting to run, in the early 1960s, a handful of years after his retirement. And like Hollywood stars back then, his remoteness – he had disappeared back into the wastelands of east Europe – only enhanced the intrigue. Because not only had he done something that no one is ever likely to emulate, winning all three distance running events at an Olympic Games, Helsinki 1952, he had done it with an exuberance and extroversion which was at odds with both his tortured running style and the propaganda which our western leaders were feeding us about the surly, joyless, mechanistic products of Soviet-bloc Communism. Speaking of which, in terms of the modern concept of soft-power, Emil Zátopek was one of the best adverts that

Communism ever had. And he was a true believer... up to a point.

Because there was a second act in Zátopek's life, which made him even more interesting. Despite being a Colonel in the Czechoslovak People's Army, when the liberalising movement of the new First Secretary, Alexander Dubček began to gather pace in early 1968, Zátopek was right in the van. He signed the 2000 Words Manifesto, which was central to the Prague Spring, and was a prominent supporter of Dubček both on the street and in the media. Then when the Warsaw Pact tanks rolled into Prague in August that year, he was one of the most vocal opponents of the 'invasion'. Not only did he address vast crowds in the streets and squares, but he was photographed haranguing Soviet soldiers on their tanks, and giving them an unusual history lesson. Had they never heard of the Olympic Truce? Did they not know, he asked, that in Ancient Greece, all battles were suspended during the extended period around the Olympic Games? And given that the Olympic Games in Mexico City were just weeks away, what were they doing here in Prague in battle dress?

It is doubtful whether the Soviet soldiers knew Emil Zátopek, any more than they knew about the Olympic Truce. Many of them were Mongolian or Tartars, the 'shock-troops' who couldn't even speak Russian. They had been told that they were going to Prague to liberate the city, and couldn't understand why they were being roundly vilified; and why the citizens had torn down all the street signs, so that none of them knew where they were going. Neither Zátopek, nor Dubček, nor any of their fellow-citizens was going to make any difference. But Zátopek didn't give up. He told an international news agency that the Soviet Union should be banned from the forthcoming Olympic Games. His role in the Prague Spring was already prominent enough, but that very public admonition for their Soviet masters was probably what saw him exiled from Prague soon afterwards, to work as a labourer for the next six years.

3.

Emil reminded me of my father, Percy - in appearance, demeanour and character. They were both jowly, as men tend to get in their seventies. They were both thin on top, and had that weathered rubicund look of the inveterate drinker. But it was the personality that struck me most. They were both lovely men, sweet and forgiving, benign characters who clearly believed that there was an intrinsic good in the world.

When Percy died, aged 89, there was no need for ceremony. For the death notice in the local paper, I wrote simply, 'A lovely man; which is why everybody loved him'. As will become clear from the numerous testimonies sketched here, Emil Zátopek was such a man. I asked many people, beginning with his widow Dana, where did it come from? Did it come from being one of the youngest in a large, country family (Percy was sixth of nine children, born on a farm; Emil seventh of eight, born in country towns)? Or what? I couldn't think of anything else, apart from natural goodness, whatever that might mean. Or was it simply a decision taken early in life not to judge? It all made me wish that I had known Emil Zátopek better.

Of course, as a journalist, I dearly wanted to find someone who would speak ill of him. And I did eventually find people, even close friends who expressed disappointment at his recanting his vociferous support for the Prague Spring. We all have our weaknesses. Nobody lives a blameless life. If anyone saw Emil Zátopek as a father figure, it was the former decathlete, TV commentator and journalist, Štěpán Škorpil. He never knew his own father. He was only 17 days old when his father, a member of the Resistance was executed in a Nazi prison camp, where he had been taken shortly after Škorpil's conception. An early 'meeting', as he termed it, with Zátopek was to have a decisive impact on his young life, in more ways than one.

"I first met Emil on the radio," Škorpil told me in early October 2014. "I was seven years old, and it was the Helsinki Olympics. I was glued to the radio. Day One, he wins the 10,000 metres, Day Three, it's the heat of the 5000 metres, then the final. The last lap, he's fourth, then he's first, then he's fourth, then (Chris) Chataway falls; and Emil wins. I was jumping up and down on my bed. The whole country must have been listening.

"You know, the only time my mother ever hit me was after this. I cut a big photo of Emil out of the newspaper, and nailed it to the wall of my bedroom. Of course, I made big holes in the wall… Many years later, I was driving Emil to a sports club somewhere, to give a talk, and I told him this story. He threw his hands up to his head (Škorpil mimicks this in the café, where we were talking), and said, 'Oh my God, you got punished because of me'. And he evidently kept thinking of this, because half an hour later, he put his hands up to his head again, then threw his arms around me, kissed me on the cheek, and said, 'My poor boy, your mother only ever hit you once, and it was my fault'. I had to say, 'Emil! Stop; or I'll crash the car' ".

I asked the obvious question, was Emil a sort of spiritual father to you? Nearing 70 at that time, Škorpil was the archetypal hard-bitten journalist, who had seen and heard of lot of things, seen a lot great performances, and heard a lot of bullshit. And he had lived through some of the most momentous events in Czech and Czechoslovak history. At 10.30 in the morning, over coffee in a bustling Prague city centre café, he almost broke down. When he gathered himself, he said, "You know, Emil once said to me, 'I am your athletics father, and Dana is your athletics mother'. That experience," he added, recalling the Helsinki radio report, "made me want to do something in sport. My father was an engineer. Who knows, if he had lived, I might have worked in factories all my life".

4.

When I told my pal Tim Johnston, who had finished eighth in the Mexico Olympic marathon in 1968 that I was going to Prague to research Zátopek, the first thing he said was, "Can you find out, once and for all, what training he actually did?" And Tim had broken one of Zátopek's records, the admittedly little run 30,000 metres on the track, in 1965. But it is symptomatic of the rumours, counter-rumours, narrative and counter-narrative that attach themselves to people like Zátopek, the more so in his case since he came from the relative obscurity and closed society of post-war Communist eastern Europe. And despite his frequent travels abroad, and willingness to chat to all and sundry in the half dozen languages he could lay his tongue on, I suspect his flamboyance and enthusiastic explanations of scarcely credible training sessions meant that it was all taken with a pound of salt. I mean to say, 100 times 400 metres, all in the same day! What sane person would or even could do that?

Even his widow Dana Zátopková didn't seem to know exactly what training he did. On my first visit to her apartment, she told me, no, the most Emil ever did was 70 x 400 metres; oh, and he never trained more than twice a day. On the table in front of her was a well-thumbed copy of their co-autobiography, published in 1960, and entitled *Dana a Emil Zátopkovi – Vypravují*, literally, Dana and Emil Zátopek Declare; or as I have seen better titled elsewhere, *As Told by Dana and Emil*. Shortly afterwards I found a copy in a second-hand bookstore in Prague city centre (and paid a student to translate it for me, since it had only ever been published in Czech and Slovak). The book is illustrated with cartoons of the couple, line-drawings typical of the period. Towards the back, during the chapter when he discusses his training, there is a cartoon featuring a sweaty Emil at trackside, and in the background a notice-board depicting 100 x 400m! Further, when I finally got a Serbian friend to translate an interview I had taped ten years earlier with the Croatian-born Franjo Mihalić, he related visiting Zlín (then in central Czechoslovakia) with Yugoslav colleagues in the mid-fifties, and watching Emil training three times in one day, and doing, yes, 100 x 400 metres.

The same conflicting stories applied to Emil's life off the track - particularly of the period when he was kicked out of the army and exiled from Prague. One person said one thing, one another. One radio chief from the sixties refused to meet me, for reasons he would not explain. More strangely, another journalist agreed to meet and then disappeared, to the extent that he stopped answering phone calls, and obviously blocked my emails, because they came bouncing back. Again, some of the stuff Dana told me proved to be, if not untrue, then different to what others remembered. Then again, she was already a 90+ year old, recalling events from up to seven decades before. And, as recent Zátopek biographer Pavel Kosatík cheerfully admitted, Emil had told his own story so many times with so many variations, additions and embellishments, it was hard to tell what the basic truth was. Evidence of that, said Kosatík, was a story Emil told of one of the two occasions when he went to the USA, and found a volume on marathon runners in a bookstore. There was a chapter on himself, said Kosatík, and he admitted that he didn't know half the stories contained there. But as any biographer or documentarist will tell you, if they are being honest, it's all an approximation anyway. Suffice to say, very soon into my research, I felt that I was engaging in some old-fashioned investigative reporting. As much as anything else, this was going to be a detective story.

5.

According to *As Told by Dana and Emil*, since he was the seventh of eight children, his parents ran out of typical Moravian or even Czech names, so, 'I got a nice French name.... out of despair. My parents felt seven of us were enough and decided I would be the last. But, they had one more baby, Jiří, two years later. It was easier with his name, because he was born on (Saint) Jiří's nameday'. Their childhood sounds like the archetypal country upbringing - playing in the streets and fields, organising games according to the season, dressing up for impromptu theatrics; getting into trouble either at school or with parents and neighbours; stealing fruit from adjacent gardens, trespassing on building sites. It was, of course a time when corporal punishment at both school and home was commonplace. Mama Zátopková, Agneška, burned papa, František's belt in the hope that it would save the kids from a burned backside, but dad had his carpenters' ruler in reserve. And when the inevitable cries of 'not me' sounded round the backyard, it resulted in a line-up so that everyone had to share in the punishment, with neighbours looking on, enjoying the show. But like his name, Emil was already employing a different style.

'I had another tactic. I didn't care about anyone seeing me crying and screaming. When we were about to get spanked, I stood at the end of the queue and when dad called 'Emil!' I started screaming and crying and I went to him as slowly as possible. I think that made him even angrier, but it ended up well for me. Dad waited patiently on his seat with the ruler in his hand. Before I got to him, there were not only neighbours' boys at the fence but also the neighbours themselves and they called out, "Mr Zátopek, don't hit him that hard, that's enough!" I think dad was so mad at that moment that he didn't even have the strength to explain I was cheating, that he hadn't hit me at all yet. For him not to look cruel though, he just hit me once on my backside and that was it. Everyone called me 'Cry-baby Emil', but it worked quite well for me.

'But there was one famous time my trick didn't work. We had excellent pears in our garden. They were beautiful but we weren't allowed to pick them. We just walked under them, smelling and testing them to see if they were ripe.

One day, I got hold of one that just came off in my hand. I hadn't intended to pick it, but when I had it in my hand I thought I might as well try it. I bit into it and it was rock-hard. What should I do? I threw it over the fence so that no one would find it, and forgot about it completely. But all of the sudden, our neighbour, Mr Riedel showed up at our door and said. "You have no idea, Zátopek, how magical your flying pears are. I was working in my garden today and – whop! There came this pear of yours, right next to me". Dad just asked his usual 'who was it?' and took up the ruler. To my horror, Mr Riedel interrupted him, "Wait a moment, you'll find out easily, there are teeth marks in the pear and as you can see, one tooth is missing in the front".

'We all had to line up and show our teeth. It was clear straightaway who did it. Nevertheless, they put the offending pear right in front of my nose, matching it my mouth. The worst thing was I couldn't use my trick in front of Mr. Riedel and start screaming in advance, so I got spanked a long, long time'.

For the rest of the time, Emil gives the impression that his principal role was that of the Artful Dodger, putting in more effort to avoid something rather than just doing it. He claims later in their autobiography that he never ran as a child, but there was one notable exception. 'With our boys' football team, I was just running around, I didn't kick the ball at all. Once I heard a comment, "That Emil is everywhere". I was glad I could add to a collective happiness at least like that, so I tried even harder to be always fresh and tireless. Who knows if I got some kind of special ability by that, ability that helped me with my athletic success later?

'Back then they put me in our football team, thanks solely to that. I ran throughout the match and ruined every game plan, even when we'd agreed on it earlier. I never scored any goals, and yet I caught the attention of our teacher by my strange way of playing. He noticed my running at the very first game I played, and after that he always sent me for his slices of ham from the butcher…

'Our Máňa saw me once and immediately told on me that I was running through Kopřivnice, tiring myself out. But nothing happened. Dad didn't say a word, because it was for the teacher, but my brothers looked at me suspiciously, because they didn't believe I could run so fast. They wanted to check it right away. They found a circuit about a kilometre long around our houses and decided we would all run together to see who could make it without stopping. I felt so fresh and able that I ran a second lap without stopping. Then on the third and fourth laps even my older brothers looked at me with admiration which was very unusual. They even offered me some refreshment. I bravely refused and ran two more circuits just to show it wasn't a problem for me.

'Soon after that all the boys in Kopřivnice knew about my endurance. Though he was two years older, Zdena Galia issued a challenge for me to race him later that week. "We´ll run to those oaks in the field and back," he said. It was about two kilometres and I was right behind him the whole time. I was just sorry I wasn't able to run a little faster, and get in front, even for a short time. After we came back, Zdena said, "Okay, so he can run". That was enough for other boys to acknowledge I made it through the test. So, as you can see, I began running as a school boy. Fortunately I stopped running shortly after that. I learned later that it's not good for a youngster to begin with long distance at 13 or 14, but I didn't know it back then'.

6.

Every great long distance runner I have met during my time in international athletics, now stretching more than fifty years, has been an obsessive. The less perceptive demonstrate their obsession by the expedient of the hours of daily training that they dedicate to their favourite pursuit. The more perceptive, like Olympian Tim Johnston, will freely admit, had it not been running, it would have been something else. Nor does it dissipate, at least not for some. Now in his mid-sixties, former 10,000 metres world record holder, Dave Bedford celebrated his partial withdrawal from the mundane tasks of the London Marathon office in 2014, by starting to run to work and back again, as he had first done as a teenager. "I had to stop," he said, shaking his shaggy head dismissively over a pint in one of our favourite Hampstead watering holes. Before I could even ask, he explained with a shrug, "the old obsession".

For someone who would work his way up to running one hundred laps of the track in just over a minute each, with a brief interval jog in between, all in the same day, the term 'obsessive' might have been coined expressly for Emil Zátopek. But he pulled every schoolboy trick he could muster to avoid running his first race as an adult. It was May 15, 1941. He was no longer a schoolboy, but an apprentice at the Bata* shoe factory in Zlín, the birthplace of such diverse 'celebrities' as British playright Tom Stoppard (né Tomáš Straussler), and Ivana Zelníčková, aka Trump. The Bata apprentices, both from Zlín and the neighbouring towns' satellite factories were so numerous that a whole social programme was dedicated to their well-being; which also served the beneficial purpose of satisfying the Nazi supervisors during this period that the youngsters were engrossed in something less dangerous than assisting the Resistance. On that score, Zátopek, in the co-autobiography with Dana, doesn't shrink from recording the toll of weekly disappearances from the factory floor.

He also recalls the active life back home, including street races, of any country boy, making him fitter than the average youngster. But he doesn't think it makes him any better than his peers at Bata, and he admits to a serious lack of interest. 'I saw some boys from the dormitory ran faster than me so I knew my abilities didn't mean a thing in this environment.... I wasn't running anymore, I didn't play football and I didn't want to see the real athletic races. I didn't even attend the *Run Through Zlín*, which was a (1400 metres) race organized especially for us.... I never even thought of trying it myself. Then an interesting thing happened to our dormitory.... I got a supervisor who told us everyone who wasn't hurt had to run. The knee that I'd knocked in the factory started to hurt immediately. He told me to go to the doctor's. But the doctor was a Bata man too, so he said I was healthy and could run. I didn't want to ruin my non-running tradition that last year. When the race day came, I disappeared to the library before everyone started to get ready for the race. I opened my chemistry books and started reading, but began to think about the race – whether the boys were back yet or not.... All of the sudden there was the captain of our team who came to me, "Don't you know you're supposed to be at the start?"

'There was no time to argue. I took my running shoes and before I got to the start line, I was warmed-up. You can imagine how annoyed I was. For so long I didn't want to run, and now I looked like I was chicken. My supervisor gave me a dirty look. The thought of winning crossed my mind. He'd be so surprised! Does he know I ran as a little boy? Then the gun fired and off we went. Right from the start I ran with the leaders, and I even got ahead of them a little bit. It went really well. I tried to breathe a lot and maybe that was the reason why I didn't feel tired. We were about half-way round when I started to feel tired.... (Honza) Krupička, started to speed up and he began to get away from me.... I put all my efforts into it, but I couldn't catch Krupička. I finished second, defeated. Then I saw my supervisor standing near the finish line, and remembered my secret wish to win the race. But he turned to me with unexpected interest, "You're Zátopek, right?" and before I had a chance to answer he told his colleagues: "There you go, that's my boy! See the effort I put into them! What a great success, can you see?"

'But was it really such a success to lose?'

Having won a fountain pen for this first effort, the following week Zátopek was told by his supervisor to select a team for a company relay competition. But when his colleagues let him down, the supervisor lost interest as quickly as he had found it the previous week. Another week later, without any demur by now, having evidently caught the running bug, Zátopek ran another company race, a 1500 metres in the Czech second city of Brno. He beat his first vanquisher Krupička, but lost to another local boy, 'Slavík from Židenice'. But now he had a track time he could conjure with, four minutes, 21 seconds for 1500 metres. For a late teenager in wartime, who probably had not been properly nourished for years, this was a notable achievement. Before winter set in, and nobody ran in winter in Czechoslovakia in those days, not even international athletes, Zátopek got the opportunity to run and train with some of the established regional athletes.

He was hooked.

---

* In using the international form of the name Bata, I am following the example of Polish writer Mariusz Szczygieł in his instructive and highly entertaining *Gottland: Mostly True Stories from Half of Czechoslovakia*. The company founder's name was Tomáš Baťa, pronounced Batya.

7.

Every interview is an adventure, but I was particularly looking forward to talking to Jindřich (Jindra) Roudný, who was a training partner of Zátopek from the earliest days, at the Bata factory in Zlín. Whereas Zátopek could only finish second in his debut, the *Race Through Zlín* in 1941, Roudný had won the event two years later. Roudný would become one of Zátopek's closest friends and acolytes, and would be the second best distance runner in Czechoslovakia, and a European champion, in the steeplechase in Brussels 1950, when Zátopek won the 5000/10,000 metres 'double'. Given that they met in that formative period of their late teens/early twenties, trained and partied together (as much as was possible during the Occupation), and that Roudný got to know the whole Zátopek family, he probably knew the Olympic legend better than anyone.

Dana had told me that Roudný was a virulent anti-Communist, who had got into a lot of trouble with remarks he had made about Stalin at the time of Uncle Joe's death in 1953. But that wasn't the only incident that had got Roudný into trouble with the authorities, as he was to relate. Ninety years old when we met, Roudný had been born in Bohemia, but when he was two his father, a tradesman, had moved to Moravia, to help build the expanding Bata factory in the 1920s. Roudný still lived in Moravia, not far from Zlín, and I wavered between hiring a car and getting the train, but settled on the latter after seeing the extensive road works on the eastbound highways on a previous trip to Olomouc.

Despite two changes of train, at increasingly smaller stations, everything synched perfectly. I arrived right on time in Zlín, and got a taxi for the last few kilometres east to Roudný's home in a converted farmhouse on the edge of the countryside in the community of Želechovice nad Dřevnicí. A few kilometres from the border with Slovakia, it is a beautiful region, with rolling, wooded hills, which graduate towards ski country. Perfect for cross country running, I thought as successive trains took me closer and closer to our meeting.

A tall, cadaverous man with a stoop and leaning on a stick was waiting for me with his dog in front of the old farmhouse. Despite his four score and ten, apart from a little deafness, he was just as bright and coherent as Dana Zátopková, who was almost two years older. "Yes," he agreed, "it is beautiful running country. We used to go with other runners, Emil and I, into these hills around here, and in the woods".

Like Zátopek, Roudný had joined the army after his Bata apprenticeship. But when the Communists took over in 1948, he found it hard, he said, to disguise his distaste for them. Though he was one of the world's best distance runners during the period when he was training regularly with Zátopek, his superiors noted in a memo, which he saw lying on his CO's desk, 'Not sufficiently politically motivated'.

As reigning European champion, he was expected to get a medal in the Olympic steeplechase in Helsinki 1952, but he didn't even qualify for the final. To make matters worse, on the training track the week before, he had shown the little-rated American Horace Ashenfelter how to take the water-jump properly, a fact that was noted subsequently, with thanks to Roudný in the US magazine *Track & Field News* when Ashenfelter won gold, beating the outstanding favourite Vladimir Kazantsev of Russia. Roudný proudly showed me the accolade in his dog-eared copy of the magazine.

But well before the Czechoslovak authorities saw the US magazine, the word had already got round in Helsinki about Roudný's water-jump seminar. A hastily convened committee, including the secret police 'minders' who accompanied the team, determined that Roudný would have no further foreign trips, having helped engineer the defeat of the Russian 'brother', Kazantsev.

But things might have been much worse, if the Czechslovak authorities had discovered that Roudný was actively considering defecting in Helsinki. The Soviet Union had turned down the invitation to attend London 1948, so Helsinki was their first appearance, but one of the provisos was that the countries of the Soviet bloc were housed separately, in Otaniemi, 25km from the Finnish capital. In the two years prior to Helsinki, Roudný had struck up a correspondence with the US 10,000 metres runner (and subsequently respected athletics writer) Fred Wilt, who was also an FBI agent, as was Ashenfelter.

"Before I went to Helsinki, I got a letter from my friend Fred Wilt, saying if I got the Middle School certificate, I could get a stipend, and choose any university I wanted in the USA. So I said (to the minders) I had to go and train in Helsinki, but I never trained, I had to speak with Wilt. I went to the American building, and there was a big African guy on the door, and I said is Fred Wilt here, he said he's gone out, and he gave me a chewing gum. I went to the training place, and Fred came with his wife. He asked me what I wanted to do. I said I have no passport, no documents, because we couldn't have them with us, and I was one year married, so I don't know if my wife can come, I think I can't do anything. There is also my mother, my sister and brothers, maybe they would have big problems, they wouldn't have work".

But it wasn't long before Roudný was busted for good. When Stalin died the following year, the news was soon on the military grapevine, but Roudný wrote to his wife (living nearby in Zlín) for confirmation. 'Is it true,' he told me quoting his letter, 'that the Bluebeard in the East has kicked off his boots?' (the English slang equivalent would be 'popped his clogs,' and when Dana first told me this story, she could not stop laughing at the memory of Roudný's *lèse-majesté*).

But it could not have been more serious at the time. "They opened the letter, and the whole year, they were looking for me to make a mistake," said Roudný, "because they couldn't arrest me without saying they opened my letter. And Emil was against this, he was very angry that they opened my letter. There was to be a meeting in Bucharest, and we were all gathered in the hotel (in Prague) before leaving, and at midnight, they woke me up. I had to go to a meeting. I went downstairs, and there were at least ten men I didn't know, with the trainer. They told me the Ministry of Defence wouldn't give me the visa to Romania, I should go to breakfast at five in the morning, I shouldn't speak to anybody, and instead of the bus, I should go back to the club.

"The same thing happened with a meeting in Warsaw. It was the Monday before Christmas they threw me out of the army, the national team, and so on. I couldn't find a job for months, nobody would give me work. I don't know how they did it, but everywhere I went, to the rubber factory, to the machine shop, there was no work for me. The father of my wife was a Communist, and he was working in a ministry, he came and cried they would send me to Jáchymov (uranium mine). There were the political prisoners in the mines (including his former running colleague Ladislav Kořán, and the world champion ice-hockey squad). This would have broken my family, but a director of a factory, a friend of my father called me. He said you are clever Jindra, you have to begin again with your hands, as a normal worker, as a labourer in the Bata factory. But a lot of people came to help, and they put me into a room where I was controlling the drawings".

Clearly an intelligent and well-educated man, Roudný eventually graduated to being principal writer/translator in English and German of technical documents for the company. He still spoke excellent English, with the inevitable hesitations which accompany a 90 year old memory. There was only one caveat. I don't know whether there was anything in what I felt was a relatively anodyne line of questions, but he seemed to get increasingly cold as the interview wore on. Maybe it was mention of another Zátopek colleague and training partner, Lada Kořán who Roudný had obviously never liked, disparaging his qualities as runner, and wondering aloud why Dana paid such attention to him on his visits from California. Whether this was some residual jealousy of Kořán's late life proximity to the Zátopeks I could not glean, and neither wanted nor needed to go there. So we finally got onto his illustrious friend.

"Emil came to Zlín in 1937, before the war. He had to work for four years in the factory as an apprentice, then he could study two years, and take an exam to go to High School, and he made it. Emil was very intelligent, but primitive, a real country boy. There were eight brothers and sisters, so he had to work a lot to make an impression in his big family. When he was young, he had this very high voice; they called him 'wimp' (he used the term 'fňutr', which took me a while to pin down – it basically describes an animal of indeterminate gender). He was very tiny, and the boys didn't want to play with him. He tried to show himself that he was a boy or a man. He was pulling the other boys and girls on the sledge, doing everything to show that he was a man. He wanted to show that he was the best, it was in his character. He was very intelligent, not like a normal boy.

"As he was studying these last two years, he was in a dormitory where they could eat, study, and there was a kitchen. And he found out that there was a maid from the chairman of the company who went with a pot for food for the dog, called Sunny. Emil found this out, got the same type of pot as her, went to the kitchen and said, 'for Sunny'. So we got food. We managed this a few times. At this time, there was not enough food, we were always hungry, and once in this dining room, they had soup with beans. We could get a bit of meat, but we had to have a card for that, but this soup was free. So we'd always had at least three lots of soup. And after three hours we went training, and we were competing in farting. Every step, one came out. We had to have some fun to get through this training.

"We had textile shoes with very thin soles, but in winter, in the ice, when it was freezing, we ran in football boots. Once Emil got an ankle injury, and he had to go to the hospital, and when he came back, he began to train slowly. He went once with our group, and we always went through a garden, and there was this big German shepherd dog, and we always went very slowly; and Emil said, 'What are you doing?' He went to the gate, and the dog was making a big noise, so he pissed on his nose, and the dog ran away".

8.

Emil Zátopek did not invent interval training, but he did develop it to what even he admitted at the end of his career was an absurd degree. Interval training – alternating fast bursts of speed with slower recuperative jogs - has probably existed since competitive running began; the Swedish development called *fartlek* (speed-play) – enlivening a steady run with faster bursts as the feeling takes you – is another version. Zátopek's 1940s training partner Jindra Roudný told me that their advisor, Dr Haluza had got his ideas of interval training from "the Americans, university coaches". But I don't know if this was post-Occupation antipathy to all things German. Because it is generally accepted (by the few people who care about these things) that the pseudo-science of interval training was developed in the mid to late 1930s Germany, and is associated with Waldemar Gerschler, who used such methods to coach Rudolf Harbig to a world 800 metres record of 1min 46.6sec, which took over a second and a half off the previous record, in 1939. (Gerschler was also an influence on the Austrian Franz Stampfl who coached Roger Bannister to the first sub-four minute Mile).

It seems that Gerschler favoured 100 and 200 metres repetitions, which makes eminent sense for 800 metres runners. But the classic 'session' for middle and long distance runners has long been accepted as 400 metre reps, one lap of a standard sized track. So let me expand on something I mentioned earlier. In an interview with Zátopek contemporary, Franjo Mihalić in the early 2000s, when I was doing some work with the Belgrade Marathon, the Croat recalled being invited by Zátopek, following a meeting elsewhere in Czechoslovakia, to spend some time in Zlín. One day, Mihalić and his Yugoslav colleagues watched astounded as Zátopek ran 100 times 400 metres in three training sessions - "Thirty at breakfast time, thirty before lunch, then forty between 4 and 6pm". The only concession to sanity that Mihalić could attest to was the pace of the 400s, "around 70-72 seconds, with 100, 150 metres jog recovery, but always in motion. We were holding our heads in disbelief. At that time, we would do ten, fifteen, twenty repetitions maximum, (at) 61-62 seconds a lap".

I have a hunch that Zátopek pulled this stunt on his erstwhile and potential rivals, in order to put them off.... and doubtless succeeded. Mihalić told me he managed to beat Emil in a small domestic race in Czechoslovakia, but I can't find any evidence of that. The major occasion he did beat him was in the Melbourne Olympic marathon, when Mihalić finished second to Alain Mimoun, and Zátopek was sixth, a few weeks after a hernia operation.

Dr Haluza (whose nickname was 'Ali') may have advised him for little more than a year, but Zátopek gives his elder contemporary full credit for providing a blueprint for when he began to develop his own ideas. In the co-autobiography with Dana, he writes. 'It was only in the following year, 1942, that I knew what proper athletic training actually looked like: around two kilometres to warm up, twenty minutes of various exercises, three fast straights and then the main content, which my trainer at the time, Dr Haluza, always said was either 2 x 300 or 600 metres, or sometimes only four or five laps, without focusing on maintaining elegant form. I also ran 800 metres once. Back then, I was already interested in timings, but he rarely let me know what they were. Dr Haluza actually held me back, rather than forcing me into running. In the beginning, he only wanted me to train two or three times a week, and no more. This created a kind of hunger within me for running, and protected me from becoming sick of training in only my first full year. This was certainly the right thing to do, since during competition season we had races almost every week. In winter, we went to the gym twice a week and then we always ran for 10 kilometres along the road. Then came 1943, and Dr Haluza took another novice under his wing, and told me that I was now experienced enough to cope alone. He simply reminded me once again that what is most important is speed. Since I believed that I had somewhat of a deficiency in this basic kinetic property, I focused my training around his advice.'

Nevertheless, his natural intelligence and curiosity led him to experiment. In an interview with Lamberto Artiolo for the Milanese weekly magazine, *Il Tempo* in 1954, Zátopek gives the best account I've found of one of his early, more outlandish examples. 'I've always wanted to know the limits of my physical resistance. I remember that when I was a boy, to get to work at Zlín, I had to take a road bordered with poplars. I wanted to test how long I could hold my breath. Until the fourth tree! The second day

I prolonged the time by holding my breath until I reached the next poplar. I continued thus, and one day I decided to hold my breath until I reached a large clump of trees at the end of the road. I ran fast, holding my breath back in my lungs. For hundreds of metres, I felt that my chest was on the verge of bursting. I seemed to be suffocating, but I did not breathe. When I reached my target, I fell to the ground and fainted.'

Apart from aberrations like that, what strikes me forcibly, looking at the training sessions detailed in *As Told by Dana and Emil* is the basic common sense of what all his early contemporaries described as a highly intelligent youngster, not a normal boy. The excess would come later. He prefaces several references to his early training, with phrases such as, 'Rome wasn't built in a day,' and, 'No one can reach the tenth floor of a building with a single jump,' cautioning against overdoing it too soon, probably the best single piece of advice for anyone starting out to train seriously.

When Dr Haluza left him to his own devices, Zátopek was still concentrating on 10 x 100 or 200 metres repetitions, with occasional forays into six x 400 metres, with 10k road runs to back up the track work. He continued that in 1944, but with variations to stave off boredom. 'I didn't have a stopwatch (but) I achieved roughly these sorts of times - 100 metres in 13 seconds, 200 metres in 26-28 seconds, and 400 metres in 55-60 seconds..... It's interesting that even fast sprinting like this allows you to cultivate great endurance. In order to maintain a fast start and finish for my races, I came up with a different combination, eg 2 x 200 + 2 x 400 + 2 x 200 metres, or 2 x 100 + 2 x 200 + 300 + 2 x 200 + 2 x 100 metres. When I did this, I also jogged for the same distance after each sprint. I finished the season as the (national) record holder for the 2000, 3000 and 5000 metres.'

In addition to the general conditioning afforded by joining the army the following year – and doubtless a better diet, following the Occupation – Zátopek doubled the amount and distance of his repetitions, but it was still nothing like his eventual training load. That was also the year, 1946, where he made his entry onto the international stage, finishing fifth in the European Championships 5000 metres in Oslo. For the next year's winter preparation after joining the Army Academy for officer training, he again sought variety, of terrain this time, to keep himself alert. 'There was an indoor riding paddock at the Academy; for horses, that is, but no one was angry when athletes showed up there as well. Everyone wondered why I bothered with heavy boots in deep sand, when wearing running shoes on the track was easier. But the increase in difficulty that it provided was the reason. Having to lift your sinking legs and stomp further and further was wonderful practise.... I would cover 10 kilometres at the riding paddock each evening.

'In Milovice (the Academy), I ran in heavy boots in the snow once again. Every day, I would run 10 to 12 kilometres, in minus 20 degrees; I wore three pairs of jogging bottoms so that I wouldn't be cold. Bundled up like this, when I returned from the run I would be as sweaty as if it were July. After training, there was only cold water available; so cold, even, that icicles hung from the taps in the washroom. I would always move the hose into place and tie it so that a huge blast of water shot out into the middle of the washroom. When I jumped into the blast, steam would rise from my skin. Friends were scared that I would catch some sort of ailment. But after training, I was always so hot that absolutely nothing could cool me down. On the contrary – I felt the way that Finns do when they go straight from the sauna to the cold lake.

His growing celebrity did not exempt him from critical banter from his colleagues, and though he reprimands himself for being annoyed at the sort of catcalls that myself and colleagues would still endure 15 years later – 'mind the matchstick!' and, more cuttingly, 'you'll never make it,' he sought refuge in the forests nearby the Academy; and yet turned that to his advantage. 'I didn't even want to go to the stadium the next day. On my way to the forest I ran as fast as I could to warm myself up five times 150 metres. On another longer soft path, I did 20 x 400m and then again five x 150m to finish. The third day I ran 20 x 250m again, but to make it more fun I ran every third effort with the longest steps that I could manage. The fourth day I ran 20 x 400m and I bounded every third one because of the (surface) bounce. On odd days I ran 20 x 250m and in the others 20 x 400m. This training really helped me. I was practicing speed, endurance, strength of my bounding and even strength of my stomach muscles, because I was running in heavy army boots. I was also resting in the wonderful natural surroundings and saving my legs on the soft grass.

'I trained in the forest like that for two months and I broke my 3000m record with the time 8min 13.6sec, in my first race of the season. Soon after that the first year of the Memorial Evžen Rošický was held in Prague. On the Friday night we had night training with tanks, but I made up for the lost sleep on the night before the race. I even slept on the Sunday morning so that I was well prepared for the competition. I was worried that I wouldn't be strong enough in the presence of the Finns Koskela and Heinström, and the Swede Nyberg. While I was worried about them, it seems they were worried about keeping up with me. I ran away from them after five (of 12 and a half) laps and finished a long way ahead, in 14.08.2, another national record and also the world's best (5000m) performance of the year'.

'In preparation for the Olympic 10,000 metres (1948), I broadened my training and created a typical routine of five x 200, 20 x 400 and five x 200 metres, with 200 metre jogs in between. I couldn't find the courage to jump while running, as I had done in the forest. In the dark, it's dangerous, and besides this, on the hard track I preferred not to jump as high, so as to avoid ruining my Achilles tendon. In the Olympic 10,000, I only needed to run 200 metres as a sprint. In the 400 metres, I achieved a time of probably somewhere between 65 and 70 seconds. In the winter, when I trained in heavy boots and hot clothes, I was understandably slower. There was a bit of a compromise in speed, but, compared to that of other distance runners, my training was still of much better quality.

'At the time, athletic experts shook their head over one thing: how I wanted to use these individual 200 and 400 metre intervals to run the whole 10,000 metres. In June, however, I almost broke the world record, and within a year I had actually done it. As a result, I didn't abandon this way of training. On the contrary – I became its most passionate supporter. In October 1949, I even increased it by ten sets of 400 metres, in order to better prepare for my attempt at a new world record. Every day, I ran sets of five x 200, 30 x 400 and five x 200 metres. Only in the third week did I start to reduce the number of sets of 400 metres by ten, and to alternate training days with resting days.

'Everything turned out as I'd planned; so in 1950 I again increased my daily training routine. I ran five x 200, 40 x 400 and five x 200 metres, with 200 metre jogs in between. This increase in training started to give me unexpected anxiety. After having mastered it once, it suddenly happened that after ten sets of 400 metres I was dragging my feet. I didn't give up, though.

However, after the eighteenth, nineteenth and twentieth set of 400 metres, I suddenly felt the force again. I couldn't make it to the end, but in the last five sets of 200 metres I got going with a flat-out sprint again. I began to realise that I was experiencing the well-known phenomenon that, after a prolonged heavy load, the nervous system cannot maintain the same concentration on its performance. After a particular exertion, it starts to slow down, although this isn't permanent. A ten or twenty minute break can provide it with some relief and wake it up again, as though a new wave of energy were arriving. After more strain, the sedative effect occurs again, and one must take another break. One must not, of course, deplete one's nervous energy.'

Undeterred, Zátopek increased his reps each year until he got to 70 x 400 metres, with occasional forays into 100 x 400. Despite cutting down the number of reps and increasing the speed as a major championships approached, he describes how coaches would come and time his training sessions, and complain that he could never win titles and run records in such a fashion. It sounds like the learned studies, evoking physics and the laws of aerodynamics which determine that bees cannot possibly fly. But fly they do, as did Zátopek. The apotheosis of all his training came, of course at the Olympic Games in Helsinki, 1952, when he won the never to be repeated treble – 5000 and 10,000 metres, and the marathon. Towards the end of his dual bio with Dana, there is a satisfied footnote: 'Whereas, in 1947, I didn't know any other long-distance runner who would run connected or repeated sets of 200 or 400 metres, today I don't know one who doesn't run them'.

However, just about everyone I spoke to – training partners, commentators, journalists and, ultimately himself agreed that Zátopek had overdone the interval training to a remarkable degree. Added to which, the unfeasibly heavy racing programme, which can only be described as Stakhanovite, forced on him as it was by a Communist regime, which basked in the propaganda value of his success, left him a lesser athlete than he otherwise might have been. I have little doubt that a more cautious approach to racing (if not to training) would have resulted in Zátopek running far better/faster than he did. Statistically speaking, his 5000 metres world record (13.57.2), run near the end of his career barely bettered that of Gunder Hägg, set over a decade earlier; and though he set five 10,000 metres world records, ending with a best of

28.54.2, his training should have resulted in a 10,000 metres record at least half a minute faster.

In contrast, take the example of Haile Gebrselassie, the ultimate inheritor of the Zátopek flame. As far as I can determine, Haile never ran more than three 10,000 metres races in any season. The most races at any distance that the Ethiopian ever ran in a season was eighteen, in both 1993 and 1998. In the former, a year after his breakthrough, thus when he was establishing himself, he ran three 10,000m and six 5000m races. In a career at the top lasting 20 years, a season's programme was usually ten to a dozen races. There could be no better example of the proceeds of caution. In Zátopek's best season, 1950, he ran 32 races, winning them all. In the two seasons following his first Olympic victory, in London 1948, he ran twelve 5000s and eleven 10,000s in 1949; and the following year, he ran twenty 5000s and seven 10,000s. Many of those races were run in the old two-day, two-nation events, eg Czechoslovakia v Hungary, thus he would run 5000 metres on Day One, and 10,000 metres the following day. I feel exhausted just writing this. According to Czech biographer Pavel Kosatík this daunting competition programme was largely the result of pressure from the regime and the army, keen to exploit their ace for their own purposes. As early training partner Lada Kořán remarked acidly of the announcement of Zátopek's trio of Olympic victories in Helsinki, "They saw it as Communism winning three gold medals, which is bullshit of course".

In an interview with Harold Abrahams (the 1924 Olympic 100m champion) for *BBC Radio* in 1967, a decade after his retirement, Zátopek is more explicit than I have seen anywhere else of the error of his ways. In response to the question, 'Do you think that some people train too much nowadays... they run 100, 150 miles a week some of them,' Zátopek replied, 'Oh yes, I did it also. My maximum was 50 kilometres in the day, 350 kilometres in a week, about 200 miles. But it is not the best. Only to run, only to make result in the number of kilometres, in the quantity of training, it is wrong. It must be also something of high quality, and not only kilometres and kilometres, miles and miles of running.

'It was maybe also my wrong way, as I was used to running 20 x 400 metres every day. Next year, I try to run 30 times, next year, 40 times, 50 times, 100 times 400 metres in one day. And then I was not able to run more, and was useless to run less. And I felt, maybe it is the limit for everybody, it's not possible to run more. But the time came, other coaches came and told me, Emil, look, Chataway, Pirie, everyone is better than you, and nobody is running so much as you are running. And it was a great lesson for me, and I asked, how is it possible? Because it is necessary to develop training; and they told me, it means not to develop quantity, it means to develop the quality of training, and to run maybe 20 times 400 metres, and the next year, again 20 times, but more fast, next year, same quantity of training, but faster than before'.

Though he would occasionally run on trails measured out in the forest, the vast majority of Zátopek's training was on the track. In the winter, he would even scatter lime on the bends so he could see where to turn in the dark. He told me, and I have seen it mentioned elsewhere, that when he did his repeat 400 metre laps, up to a maximum of 100, he ran them in lane six of the track. Due to what are known as lane 'staggers' he could use the spare 40 metres from the finish line to his start point as his recovery jog. Another point he insisted on, and it's something that Mihalić remarked the day he and his Yugoslav colleagues watched Zátopek run 100 x 400 metres. "I never stopped, I never took a pause".

9.

The liberation of Zlín by the Soviet Army in May 1945 would soon offer Zátopek a major opportunity to assure his future both socially and athletically; that is, if he didn't get shot in the final skirmishes with the German occupying forces. As usual, he'd been training on the bomb-cratered track at Zlín, and noticed that several colleagues had left their tracksuits in the stadium changing rooms. With pretension to immortality that only the young enjoy, he delivered the garments to their owners during exchanges of fire between the advancing Russians and retreating Bosch.

'I almost didn't get to Kantůrek's, because the street in front of their house near the church was under the direct fire of the Soviet guns. It was accompanying the last German vehicles driving away down the main road. I used a break in the convoy and I ran to some front door. Scared inhabitants were reluctant to open up. But when they saw it was only me, carrying old and dirty tracksuits they looked quite happy. Then I ran through the streets straight to Kůty's, then to Zdráhal's. Of course they didn't believe me that there was firing by the church. We looked from the window – and there were soldiers running around the school in Zálešná St, but they weren't German.

"It's the Soviets! Finally they're here".

'We all jumped with joy, and were beside them in a flash. What a welcome there was, with hugs and embraces; people brought food and drink, and the excitement just went on and on. We spent days with them. We looked at their guns, and asked all kinds of questions, just like they did. After a week I knew enough to join the army myself. When I mentioned this to the older athletes, that I thought I'd like that kind of life, they were all against it'.

So were his employers at Bata, though they had nothing but hard work to offer as alternative. And potential silicosis, since at that time, he was working in a section smashing silicates for experiments. Despite having set three national records the previous year, the company personnel officer refused him time off to go to a championship in Prague. When he complained, he was threatened with a company disciplinary camp. The decision was more or less made for him. He took the shilling.

'It was a better move than I'd expected,' he later wrote. 'Training in the forest every day, morning gymnastics, marches and running; training from the morning to the evening. I even liked the early wake-up call, because I found it stiffened my will, self-control and toughness. I didn't miss any of the fight or night training and I did all of the exercises with the same enjoyment as I ran my two hundreds (metres) on the track. When I went training in the stadium in the evening, others were surprised I hadn't had enough after a full day. But my efforts paid off; I celebrated the first (post-war) Czechoslovak Championship with a new 5000m record, 14min 50.8sec.

'After coming back to barracks I went to hear the daily orders with my platoon and I was curious to see what was new. To my surprise the commander complimented me in front of the whole platoon for my excellent sports performance. I really hadn't expected such interest. I told myself, the army is a great thing for sportsmen, and that I wouldn't ever swap my uniform for Civvie Street again. I signed up for the army academy, and before I became a commissioned officer I achieved some major successes.'

10.

By popular consent, Sydney Wooderson looked the antithesis of the world class athlete. Spindly arms and legs, and a weedy frame engulfed in black baggy shorts and black running vest (the uniform of his south London club, Blackheath Harriers). With his 'short-back-and-sides' and wire-rimmed specs he looked exactly like what he was, a mild-mannered solicitor. But boy, could he run! He was one of the very few men to concurrently hold world records for both middle distance events, in his case the Half-Mile and Mile (1937/8), and he extended his post-War career to 1948, in order to train for what at the time was the most hotly contested cross country race in the world, the nine miles (15k) English 'national'. He won that too. Two years earlier he was one of the favourites for the European Championships 5000 metres, in Oslo, Zátopek's first major international race.

In respect of Wooderson, Zátopek was no different to anyone else. In his co-autobiography with Dana, he records clapping eyes on the slightly-built Englishman for the first time, as they lined up for the 5000 metres final in Oslo. 'I acknowledged before the start that it would be something different to what I'd known,' wrote Zátopek. 'When the most famous long distance runners showed up on the track, people started shouting. They recognized the world record holder Viljo Heino and the whole tribune (grandstand) started to chant, Hei–no, Hei–no, Hei–no…

'That's horrible, I said to myself, we're not even running yet, and they're shouting already. What is it going to look like when we run? Then there were the English from the other side, with, Woo–der–son, Woo–der–son… I guess they trusted their favourite. I'd also heard several times myself that he might actually win this race. I paid close attention when the starter called us to the line, so that I'd know which one he was. After a few famous and unknown names, there was Wooderson – a small, serious man, wearing glasses showed up on the line. He had shorts down to his knees, and he looked more like a bank clerk than a world record holder. I wondered if it wasn't just a joke, him being the favourite.

'After a frantic start that I hadn't experienced before, I saw him together with the ones at the back. It was a mistake about him, I thought, and I began to chase the leaders. We were fighting over the leading position so much that no one could raise the pace anymore. In the last lap, Wooderson just flew around us like the wind, and I was glad to finish fifth. I ran 14min 25sec, breaking my old record by 11 seconds. But what kind of a success was it if I didn't win? After we returned to Czechoslovakia, everyone said, "You didn't have to go to Norway to finish fifth, you can do that at home".'

The reception at his next major event, immediately afterwards, was no kinder. Thousands of people at the Allied Forces' Championships in Berlin two weeks later treated Zátopek as a joke. Since he was the only athlete of note in the Czechoslovak military he travelled alone, and arrived late, having been misdirected on his first solo trip outside the country. He had to persuade the organisers, who had already compiled the entry lists that he was bona-fide; and the march-past at the opening ceremony was equally contentious. When the American soldier carrying the CZECHOSLOVAKIA sign discovered that there was 'just one', according to Zátopek, he treated the athlete dismissively. As did the 70,000 crowd, who laughed out loud at the sight of a solitary figure no more robust than Wooderson following the throngs of other countries' representatives. The laughter only intensified when the gun for the 5000 metres went, and Zátopek shot off and built up a huge lead within the first two or three laps. But the laughter soon evaporated when he kept going, and won by the proverbial street. At the closing ceremony, Uncle Sam came looking for him and, as Emil wrote: 'This time he made up for everything that he hadn't done at the start. We both marched proudly, and the crowd applauded loudly'.

11.

The other Zátopek contemporary from the 1940s that Dana put me in touch with was Ladislav (Lada) Kořán who, unlike Roudný did *not* avoid a lengthy incarceration in Jáchymov, the uranium mine cum prison camp. But Kořán, who ended up living in California, where he was known as Larry, had a life well worthy of documentation. Though an excellent junior runner, he had a parallel life as an electronics engineer, earning himself the title of 'Father of the Czech Electric Guitar'. He claimed the Beatles used his guitars, and indeed I found a picture of George Harrison in his early days with a Gracioso Futurama from Kořán's Resonet company. His business acumen quickly made him a leading suspect of the Communist regime and after some misadventures, including an abortive 'escape' with his family to Germany, during which a friend was killed, he ended up in Jáchymov for over a decade. Even when he was released he couldn't get work so had to go back to Jáchymov as a paid electrician. He finally got out of Czechoslovakia during the brief liberal honeymoon which followed the Prague Spring. But he didn't sit still and enjoy the freedoms of California. He went on to become a marine engineer, and worked with the famous French oceanographer, Jacques Cousteau.

I originally spoke to Kořán on Skype, but arranged to meet him on his yearly visit to his home village, in south Bohemia, some 100 kilometres from Prague. However, in October 2014, he got a debilitating influenza which confined him to barracks for the whole period of my final visit to Prague that year. Undaunted at 90, he decided to come back to Czecho, as he called it, in spring rather than autumn 2015. We finally met up, at our pre-arranged venue, the famous Slavia restaurant opposite the baroque Národní divadlo (National Theatre), where Zátopek had his final send-off.

Kořán was still a stocky dynamic presence, something he credited to his second wife, Vaneesa (sic), who was 30 years younger. Kořán had been more interested in cycling as a teenager, but one of the most momentous events of the Nazi Occupation, the assassination of SS man and Hitler favourite Reinhard Heydrich by two underground agents who used bicycles to affect a getaway, would change the direction of his sporting life.

"I was only 17 years old at the time, and I was racing bicycles, and they (Nazis) banned bicycles on the road, and didn't let us do this sport any more. So I started to run. I was living in a sports village at the time. It was in the woods, and was modelled on the Hitler Jugend (Youth). And the guys said let's go running; there's nothing they can do to us. So I started to run. The first run was an eight kilometres race. There were eight of us in the club, and I came first of them, and eighth in the race, which was a big surprise. One of the men gave me a distance to run every day – I was running as a junior against the men – and after two weeks I ran again, and I won all nine races until the end of the season in the junior category. This was cross country. I didn't even know then that the main running was on the track. Then it came to my first race in the (senior) men category. That was 1943 in March; I was already 18 years old. From 80 people, I won this race, and it was big news, not only I won it, I won by 27 seconds. My uncle from Brno sent me a telegram, he'd read it in the newspapers. For me, track and field, or athletics was my life then, all through the Occupation.

"On the track I ran 1500 metres and 5k, but mainly 1500 metres. Then springtime and fall I was running cross country. And 1945, in November, first Sunday in November, I founded a race in the north of Bohemia, in Teplice, it's called the *Run Around Dobravke*, there's a hill, a castle on the top, it's very nice; and in 1945, I won the first race, then I won two more, and now in November (2014) will be the 70th running of the race of Dobravke (he revived sufficiently from influenza to attend the race he founded three score and ten before).

"Emil, I saw first in 1942, in a race in Prague, for a cross country. He was the winner already then. In 1943, I moved to Slavia, one of the biggest clubs in Czechoslovakia, and I was sent to a junior championship, to a Moravian town, I don't remember the name now. And this is where I met with Emil, and somehow, from the beginning, we liked each other. And whenever he came to Prague, we got together. And we meet often after that. Since then, we were friends 'til the end.

"He was really good, I tell you, Emil was the only man in Czecho at that time who was thinking of world success, from the beginning. He did not want to run this race in Zlín (his unwilling debut). They made him run it, because he was in the school of Bata, but when he did – he was second in that first race, and there were a lot of people running – and so he found out that he can do it. And he from the very first moment was thinking about how to improve in racing. We were together in the military, in the same camp, we were training together. It was the second year of this military academy, tank regiment. He was already a lieutenant, because he was a professional soldier. We spent the whole winter of '46/'47 together, training together. I was one whole month, training on the skiing and came back, and I was training really hard, but somehow from the deep snow, when we went for the first training, I had the power but I did not have the speed that I had before. So we went to the study afterwards, and he told me what to do. Don't run now with me, he said, at least for a week or two. Go to the soccer stadium, and run from one goal to the other, with long steps, just jumping (bounding), to completely relax the whole stiffness that I had from the deep snow. So I did that, and we trained again together, and then I came to Prague, because they told me to run a race, which I had won in 1943 already, and this was 1947. And I won the race, with fifty good long distance runners of Czechoslovakia then. I won by three and a half minutes.

"He coached himself, there was nobody knew so much about it as him, because he did it according to his experience himself from running. Nobody was running the interval training then, 200 (metres) fast, 200 slow. And 50 times! That was incredible back then. This race in Prague was qualification for an Allied Forces championship race in Hannover".

Despite its geographical location in the ambit of the Soviet Union, for a brief period after the war, Czechoslovakia remained close to the west. The Government in Exile, headed by President Edvard Beneš had been based in London during the War, and the fact that many Czech fighters had been stationed in the UK meant that military ties were still strong, evidence of which in the sporting arena meant that in addition to the Hanover race, which was won by the Czechoslovak squad, Zátopek and his army colleagues ran in the UK in the autumn of both 1946 and 1947, in a multi-sport competition called the Britannia Shield. When I visited him at the end of last century, that's to say, 50 years afterwards, Zátopek reeled off the sports and venues without hesitation – "The shooting was at Aldershot, the boxing at Wembley, the fencing at RAF Halton, and the cross-country on Ascot Racecourse".

Zátopek won the cross-country on both occasions by big margins from men who later featured highly in the International Cross Country, precursor to the World Cross. Fans would always regret that Zátopek never ran the 'International' as we knew it; but that was because Czechoslovakia was on the cusp of becoming a Communist ruled country. Kořán was a member of the Britannia Shield team in the second year, 1947. Although the bloodless parliamentary coup, known as 'Victorious February' was still six months away, it became clear to him that institutions were already being infiltrated by Party members.

"They invited me to the HQ, and told me, oh, you are now leaving to England, you will be living in Uxbridge, and this and that, and we are interested in this and this and this. And when you come back you will tell us all you saw. And this was already in 1947, before they took power, but they already had influence. I was going to visit friends in Great Britain and I did, and when I came back I was a nervous wreck. But I didn't go, and no one came after me to say you didn't come and report to us as we told you. But they had maps, they showed me where we would land and where we should stay, they even knew the name of the Colonel in charge. I was stunned". On a lighter note, the younger Kořán had suffered badly in the race itself, and finished in a state of collapse. "The British prepared a race with fields, water, barriers, not easy to jump over. I came to the finish line exhausted, and Emil was waiting for me, and I was really somewhere else, and he grabbed me and took me to the hall, and threw me into the pool, and I woke up, he was the boss of the team, but he was taking care of us.

"If you were his friend he would give you anything he had, he didn't think of himself. Once, after we won this Hanover race, I was redirected from the tanks to the sports division of the army, and I was living in Strahov (National Stadium). I had a room and shower, everything, it was fantastic. Emil was the commander of the sports battalion in Prague, and the people from the newspapers were already after him. Sometimes he would come up the backstairs to my apartment, and nobody knew where we were. Once he came from Zlín, and remember at that time we really didn't have anything after the

War. The track was like a potato field, and we didn't have proper shoes. He was still running for Bata Zlín; and he bought a pair of tennis shoes, not for racing, but beautiful shoes, yellow rubber shoes. I said, Emil, these are beautiful, what you've got there. He said, you really like them? I said, they're beautiful; he said, so, they're yours. I said wait a minute, but we had the same shoe size, and I couldn't talk him out of it, I had to take them. He said you would not be my friend if you don't take them. So I had to take them. I should have saved them, and put them in a golden box".

12.

As with so many young Czechoslovaks in the inter-war period, Dana Ingrová's introduction to sport was with the local Sokol society. Sokol (falcon) is a cross between a gymnastic society and the Boy Scout and Girl Guide movements. It was 'invented' or developed in the Czech lands, ie Bohemia during the Austro-Hungarian Empire by a German-speaking Czech, who Slavicised his name to Miroslav Tyrš, and by a colleague, Jindřich Fügner. Sokol eventually spread throughout east Europe, and abroad, and there are still Sokol societies in the USA, where it was introduced by immigrants.

Like the German *Turnverein* movement from the early 19th century, on which Sokol was undoubtedly based, the organisation soon acquired a socio-political role, which fed in this case into Czech nationalism, one of the motors for the foundation of Czechoslovakia in 1918, when the Austro-Hungarian Empire crumbled in the wake of World War I. For the majority of the youngsters, however, Sokol was simply a vehicle for games, exercise, sporting competition and, by the time girls were permitted, when Dana began practising in the early 1930s, also an opportunity to meet members of the opposite sex.

At that stage however, Dana was clearly more interested in sport of all kinds, until the German Occupation brought everything to a halt. She writes in their dual autobiography, 'Everything changed with the war. It seemed to be the end of all sporting fun. There was all sorts of rubbish in the gym and the pretty mats disappeared. People got lost – in short, it was wartime. Back then, we had nowhere to go, but we found out Hradiště had quite a good playground where we could possibly do something. By a coincidence, there was a big handball fan in Hradiště at that time. He was the sort of guy who doesn´t just say he's going to do something; he goes out and does it. He started organizing games, with all the equipment. He begged for money from other sport fans, and he always got some, because there were plenty of them. After all, we really didn't need more than that at the beginning. I happened to be part of this team as well. I can't remember how I got in though – I think I was peeking through a fence one day and someone invited me in. Before we got to our first match, I was made captain of this new team, because I had the best aim of all the girls. Because of that, my sporting future was determined for the next seven years. We started to compete and got better and better. We certainly had enough rivals. Handball was a really popular game back then. Even small villages had their own female handball teams.'

It sounds as if Dana was something of a tomboy, remarking that her dad was annoyed that she, 'chased the ball like a fox-terrier, (and) my mom was worried that I wouldn't get married because of that, and my brothers just sighed, 'How can you enjoy that?' That only made me play handball even more'. She continued playing even after she went to her first Olympic Games in London 1948. And she was still the star player of the team which won the provincial championship the following year. But she gave up handball after that success to concentrate on a discipline that she'd only chanced on when she went to a physical education college in 1946, and began trying out various athletics events. 'At one small competition in Třeboň I just picked up and threw a javelin. I threw it with all my strength, and I got a sensational 34 metres.

'Nowadays, that may seem funny to you, but I can assure you I was written up in the newspapers, in bold text. My acquaintances asked me if it was really me. Some of them didn't believe me, because they never saw me with a javelin. My parents never even noticed, of course'. As for handball, it seems that during that period, it was generally a good training ground for throwers. Dana's first javelin idol, the Austrian Herma Bauma had also been a good handball player prior to winning the 1948 Olympic title; ditto Dana's Czechoslovak colleague, Olga Fikotová, whose handball background propelled her to winning the discus at the 1956 Olympic Games.

13.

Prior to going to Ascot for his second successive victory in the Britannia Shield, Zátopek got an opportunity to show his versatility at the World University Games in Paris in September 1947. Although he had just turned 25, because he was in the Officers' Academy he qualified as a student. The trip seems to have been as badly planned as the one to Berlin for the Military Championships a year earlier; because when he got to the French capital, he discovered that the 5000 metres wasn't for another five days. Undaunted, he decided to enter the 1500 metres, virtually a sprint for a long distance man. Yet he was more than equal to his ambition.

He won his heat easily in a personal best time of 3min 55.2sec, then in the final on the penultimate day of the championships he won the title, beating the favourite Sándor Garay of Hungary in another personal best of 3.52.8. Inevitably, he won his then speciality, the 5000 metres on the final day, in 14.20.8. But most impressive was the fashion in which he had reasoned his way to victory in the shorter race.

A dozen years later, he recalled, 'I had two options to choose from: either lose in the finishing sprint, or run away from them from the start. So I started so fast that only Hungarian Garay kept up with me. I ran the first kilometre in 2.33, which I'd never run, even in a 1000 metres race. I still heard him behind me. I was just waiting for the finish line to come and for him to outsprint me. Then I heard his steps gradually getting quieter about 60 metres before the finish. I didn't even look behind me to see what had happened to him. I ran through the finish and about a step behind me there was someone else – the Frenchman Quilici. The exhausted Garay was fifth in the end. I really was smarter than those greyhounds'.

He would do something similar during his *annus mirabilis* of 1950, when he went through the whole of a season of 32 races unbeaten. And this time it was against a future world 1500 metres record holder, his young colleague Stanislav Jungwirth. But given that Jungwirth was only 20 at the time, he may well have been overawed by celebrity. Zátopek recalls: 'We met at the national relays in Gottwaldov (formerly and later, Zlín), where we both ran the last leg for our clubs. Standa (Stanislav) was faster on paper, what's more, he got the baton 15 metres ahead of me. Everything was set up for a grand finale. I ran after him so fast that I caught him within 200 metres. Then it was me making the pace. Standa kept up until the last 300 metres, when he sped up and took the lead. It looked hopeless for me, but I didn't give up. I sprinted past on the last bend, and I crossed the line several metres ahead of him. After that, people were saying that I couldn't be defeated. And my great form didn't disappear in autumn either. There was already the first snow of the winter lying on Strahov when we had the last match against the Soviet Union. And I won again (10,000 metres) by a huge margin'.

14.

Post-War London could not have been a very prepossessing place. The city was widely pock-marked with wasteland where buildings had been destroyed during the Blitz. Food rationing was still in full force, although many other countries chipped in with supplies, and athletes were given double rations, the same as manual workers. When we met in 1998, Zátopek recalled, "It was a sad time for London. They were poor after the War and internationally, Mahatma Gandhi had just declared independence. Industry was low. It was a difficult time for Great Britain. Some people didn't even know the Olympic Games were taking place". Nevertheless, the London Olympics of 1948 must have been a marvellous experience for a newly minted couple. In her very first serious season of javelin throwing, Dana had qualified to represent Czechoslovakia at the eleventh hour, and so joined Emil on the plane out of Prague. He was one of the favourites for the 10,000, if not the 5000 metres. And they were in love, which they underlined by a trip to Piccadilly Circus at the end of the Games to buy wedding rings. There was, however the considerable hurdle of Dana's father, who just happened to be Emil's former commanding officer, the one who had congratulated him in front of the whole platoon after he had won the national 5000 metres title in record time.

Dana and Emil had met only two months prior to London, at a small athletics meeting in Zlín, where they had congratulated each other on recent records. In their co-autobiography, Emil says he took a shine to her straightaway. Shortly afterwards, they took a team coach to a meeting in Bratislava. 'He was trying to impress me the whole time,' Dana writes. 'He was doing headstands, walking on his hands, even pretending to eat ants. Then he started to show off with how many songs he knew. But with that, he found the right person. There was no one in my circle who knew more songs than me. So on our way back he used that as an excuse to sit next to me'.

Emil takes up the story, 'I was walking her home in Uherské Hradiště, where I spent the first days of my military service. We saw the old regimental commander of mine. I was going to tell her about the compliment he gave me in front of all the other soldiers after I set a record back then. But Dana got in first. "That's my dad right there," she said. "Come on, I'll introduce you". "You can introduce me to your mom," I said, "your dad and I know each other a little bit already". But this time he didn't pay me any compliments. In fact, he didn't look very happy at all'. According to Dana, her father told her, "He's a runner, he'll run away". But Emil wasn't going to be swayed from his objective. Despite burning the cakes when he tried to help out her mother in the kitchen, and failing dismally in the headstand her father had specified as a condition of his approval, Emil's open-hearted character won both parents over, and they soon gave their consent.

At one point in their book, Dana notes, 'It was easier to monitor a bag of fleas than Emil'. She was talking about his breaking the curfew on male visitors to the women's camp during the London Games, but she could equally have been talking about Emil gate-crashing the Opening Ceremony. While the weather deteriorated so badly by the time of the 5000 metres later in the week that it is hard to distinguish which mud-covered figure is Zátopek and which his vanquisher, Gaston Reiff of Belgium, the Opening Ceremony was held in a heatwave. Given that the 10,000 metres was the following, first day of competition, the Czech team leaders forbade Emil to attend the athletes' march-past.

'I was annoyed I wouldn't see the best thing,' he wrote. 'At home, everyone will ask me what the Olympic Games were like and what am I going to say? "I don't know, I was sitting in the shade". "At least, let me go to the stadium," I begged. "I'll just watch the march past, and then I'll go back. I don't have to be there 'til evening". In the end, they agreed and I went to Wembley. When everyone was lining up around the stadium, I wanted to join them but I was spotted straightaway. "Emil, go home! You have a race tomorrow, I don't want to be responsible for your failure". I was slowly going around with the Danish delegation that was behind our team. We talked a bit and inside a few moments, we were inside the stadium. Then it was easy; once through the gate, I sped up and joined the last three members of my own team. I was happy, and our coaches in the front didn't even notice. They were interested in the solemn parade in front of the British king; but when we lined up in the centre field, they quickly spotted me.

'"Who allowed you in here; how come you're not at home?" And there were more and more reprimands coming down on my head. "So what, I'm here," I said calmly. They couldn't send me away now, the king was watching, so what would it look like if I was ushered out. We took the oath, the last runner of the Olympic relay lit the flame, the pigeons were released, the flag was raised and the XIV Olympic Games were officially launched. But my indiscipline had its repercussions at the coaches' meeting that evening. "You can't punish him now," I heard Knĕnický say through the thin wall. "He'll get nervous and will lose tomorrow. And he'll blame you because he'd be unhappy that you punished him". "OK, so we'll punish him after the race".'

Emil says that the first time he heard the chant 'Zá-to-pek, Zá-to-pek,' had been at a junior relays meeting as far back as 1942, but it was in London where it really caught on. It seems that it was a common feature at that time. He mentions the chants for Heino and Wooderson at the European Championships in Oslo 1946. Two years later at Wembley, Heino was co-favourite for the 10,000 metres, but the Finn dropped out before halfway, killed off by the torrid pace set by Zátopek who went on to win by 300 metres. But it was some time before the folks back home heard the news. The race started late, and the radio time allotted to Prague ran out before the tenth lap, when Zátopek had yet to take over the lead from Heino. The race also ended in some confusion, perhaps due to Zátopek's having lapped all but two of the runners. Officials lost count of the laps that the others had done, and produced a list of finishers which included men who had dropped out before the end. It was finally cleared up, but a footnote, so to speak to the confusion is that having taken off his spikes to relax and talk to rivals and officials, when he went back to find them, the spikes had disappeared. "Yes, we don't know 'til today who did it," Dana told me. "Somebody said these spikes are now in Paris".

Since he had led from the tenth lap, the crowd had plenty of time to practise a chant that would reverberate around stadia and streets across the world for the next decade. He probably should have won the track distance 'double' but he came unstuck spectacularly in the 5000 metres, and rightly blames no one but himself. 'I got so many compliments that I started to think I was a master and that I would tear everyone apart like a frog in the 5000 metres. That much confidence can only hurt. I wanted to show off during the next race and the

42

spectators who knew me from the 10,000 metres were helping. The chant of "Zá-to-pek, Zá-to-pek" that resounded throughout the stadium made me run as fast as I could. But what I expected didn't happen. In the rain on the muddy track I didn't get the chance to run away from others and when I got tired they ran away from me. Only two of them, Reiff and Slijkhuis (Netherlands), but they were enough. I was broken. It´s gone now, I thought. I can only get the bronze. I kept ploughing through the mud, annoyed until the last lap. Then I noticed Slijkuis was slowing down. On the back straight I sped up and there I was, in front of him. Now Reiff didn't seem that far ahead anymore. I sprinted to get him. I was getting closer, metre by metre, but there was such a rumble in the stadium that it woke him up. He turned to see what was going on. A huge struggle started between us. I was faster, and was getting closer and closer, and closer. But the finish tape ended our fight before I could pass him. There was about a metre between us'. His spikes had gone missing after the 10,000 metres and so, many years later did his 5000 metres silver medal. Dana told me that, in the early sixties, after they had both retired there was a travelling national expo dedicated to the Olympic couple. The silver medal went missing in Pardubice. "We never heard of it again," she said.

Back in London in 1948, Dana and Emil had been disappointed on arrival to discover that the men and women were billeted about 20 kilometres apart, the men at West Drayton, near Uxbridge, west London, while the women were at Northwood. Despite the ban on male visits, Emil would get up most mornings at 5am, and make the 90 minute trek, via bus, tube and train to spend time with Dana, until the Draconian warden got up, and would throw him out. She probably felt even more justified in ejecting him after his visit the day following the 5000 metres.

Dana writes, 'Emil was really annoyed after his 5000 metres. He lost the gold medal by a metre, which makes you sadder than if you lost by a whole lap. And we were all counting on the second gold, and he kind of disappointed us. The next day, he came to see me in Northwood. We were sitting on the edge of the swimming pool and we were talking about how it might've ended up if he'd started his sprint sooner; if the 5000m were two metres longer, if Reiff hadn't been so fast, and so on and so on. Meanwhile, Emil was absent-mindedly playing with his only gold medal. All of the sudden it slipped out of his hands and fell into the pool. I couldn´t jump in, because I didn´t have my swimsuit. Emil didn´t have his either but men's underwear is better for such occasions, so after hesitating briefly, he jumped in. He was happy to retrieve it and no one would ever have known that he was swimming in the women's pool. But the director chose that very moment to show up, while he was taking off his underwear behind a tree. I don't know if she saw anything, but she probably did. She got really angry and she spoke loudly for a long time. We didn't understand a single word, but the ultimatum was clear; her index finger pointed to the gate, and it uncompromisingly said: Out!'

***

There were a couple of baleful postscripts to the London Olympic Games for the Czechoslovak team - portents of things to come. The first started as a joke, and indeed could have been the model for Milan Kundera's first novel of the same name. At a reception at Buckingham Palace for the gold medallists, when Zátopek was introduced to King George VI, Queen Elizabeth remarked, 'The Czechoslovak Army must be marvellous if it has such rapid officers'. The head of the Czechoslovak canoe squad Karel Popel, who was standing behind Zátopek chipped in with something to the effect that the national army officers had a reputation for running away. When he and report of his comments got back to Prague, he was relieved of his team duties and his passport.

His colleague, Marie Provazníková had more foresight. A leading light in the Sokol movement that had first introduced Dana Ingrová to sport, Provazníková defected in London after coaching the gymnastics team to gold medals. She blamed what she called 'lack of freedom' following the 'Victorious February' coup earlier that year, which had brought the Communists to power. She stayed in Britain for several months before going to the USA, where she lived for the rest of her life. She died in 1991, three years after the Velvet Revolution which saw the Sokol movement reintroduced into Czech daily life. She was 100 years old.

15.

When I was living in France in the late 1970s, and still running to a fairly high standard, I would occasionally encounter Alain Mimoun at cross country races. He was indefatigable, even more so than Zátopek. He was already in his late fifties, and would go on competing well into his sixties, and running every other day in his late eighties. I'd often want to go and say hello to him after a cross-country race; but he was always talking, or rather, holding court. The image I have is of him taking about half an hour to get back into his track suit after a race, because he'd be waving his arms, pointing his fingers, grabbing people's shoulders, the better to make his point, while declaiming non-stop on training, racing, tactics, etc. Because Mimoun, whom Zátopek called his 'shadow,' so frequently did he finish behind him, was as irrepressible a talker as the man he called both 'brother' and 'saint'.

When I finally met Mimoun properly in 2001, the more he talked the more he reminded me of the great Moroccan runner, Saïd Aouita, with whom I'd made a TV documentary in the late 1980s. They were both compulsive talkers, with a fund of anecdotes. It made me wonder if there was something in the Maghrebin character, a sort of 'Scheherazade Syndrome', which lends itself to story-telling. I'm not saying that they weren't telling the truth, but that they both told their stories with such relish, I suspected a capacity for embellishment. Like with Zátopek, it certainly made for entertaining interviews.

Mimoun was born in Algeria at the beginning of 1921, eighteen months before Zátopek. Both began running in their late teens, which would already be considered late nowadays. But because of the war - Zátopek was working for Bata in occupied Czechoslovakia, while Mimoun fought with the Allied Forces in north Africa and Italy – their international careers were put on hold until their mid-twenties. I first interviewed Mimoun for a newspaper piece, and later went back with a cameraman. We stayed the whole day at his home at Champigny sur Marne, east of Paris – so late that we missed the last Eurostar back to London that night – and heard his whole life story, with particular reference to Emil Zátopek.

"I met him for the first time, I think it was his first international race, he was invited to the big cross country event we had in Algiers. I was living in France by then, and wasn't training. I'd only just come back from military service, but they invited me as a guest. I remember meeting at a banquet beside the sea, at Surcouf. I introduced him to crevettes (prawns), he didn't know what they were. They didn't have them in Czechoslovakia at that time. Meeting him was an unforgettable experience. Our friendship was born there.

"He was a great man. Although he was born into a working class family, he was intelligent, highly intelligent. I wasn't a champion back then, but he seemed to have some sixth-sense that I could be. He got me an invitation to go to Prague the following year, 1947. I still wasn't training properly, and I finished almost a lap behind him in the 5000 metres, but he greeted me with a 'well done', so as not to discourage me. Then a year later, by the time of the Olympic Games in London 1948, I made a big breakthrough. Nobody expected me to finish second in the 10,000 metres behind my friend, but that's what happened. And it was the start of two exceptional careers".

16.

In his cult novel, *Zen and the Art of Motorcycle Maintenance*, sub-titled *An Inquiry into Values*, author Robert Pirsig spends many pages trying to dissect the concept of quality, and ultimately decides that it is indefinable. Yet Pirsig in his alter-ego of Phaedrus (Wolf) says that quality is something we instinctively recognise. During the Olympic Games in Beijing 2008, I caused a minor tremor in the athletics blogosphere when I wrote a piece criticising the hugely successful Ethiopian Tirunesh Dibaba as boring. Without regaling you with the full text, I essentially said that a woman as good as she was – three Olympic and five World Championships gold medals – should impose herself more in races where she knew she was going to win, rather than being content to dawdle behind inferior athletes, knowing she could outsprint them on the last lap. Basically, I was asking where her self-respect, her quality as an athlete was. When, inevitably, I received a welter of criticism, I responded by citing the example of a man I knew well, Saïd Aouita.

Two decades earlier, we had been at an end-of-season meeting at New Delhi. The Moroccan was nearing the end of his illustrious career, and could have contented himself with loping around the 1500 metres in something adjacent to 3min 40sec, and the unsophisticated spectators (athletics is nowhere near being a major sport in India) would have been none the wiser. But Aouita had other ideas. On a humid evening, with temperatures in the mid-thirties Celsius, he got a colleague to help him set the pace for a couple of laps, before striking out on his own, racing the final 700 metres alone, and winning by the length of the finishing straight in just under 3min 35sec. The crowd instinctively recognised they were seeing something special, and rose to cheer him to the echo. At the meeting hotel later, I asked him why he had bothered to put in so much effort, when a sprint in front of the grandstand would have produced the same result. He replied, "When the crowd pays to see Aouita, they deserve to see the real Aouita".

The great Australian distance runner Ron Clarke emphasises this notion of quality (or class in modern parlance) elsewhere in this book. But I was gratified to come across the following passage in *As Told by Dana and Emil*. As mentioned in the previous chapter, Mimoun had come to Prague for the first time in 1947, after their initial meeting in Algiers the previous year. Zátopek recalls. 'I won the 5000 metres in 14min 15sec and finished over half a lap ahead of Mimoun. A French journalist Marcel Hansenne* didn't understand. "Why do you run so fast and try so hard since you could win with an average performance?" "Because I want to learn how to run, not prove myself smarter than the rest. Why would I slow down when I know I can get a better time if I run harder?" That's how I answered, but I'm not sure he understood. I didn't understand the suggestion that I should win a race tactically and not be tired at the end; or that I should run behind a rival and then show off by sprinting at the finish. I never minded that I got tired in a race. It's actually the precise opposite. I felt that I was justifying all the training I'd been doing'.

* This is a bit of a curiosity, because Zátopek was a student of the sport as well as an arch-competitor. Elsewhere he cites numerous examples of minor medallists and their foibles. Yet he seems to ignore that though Hansenne wrote for *L'Équipe*, he was still a practising athlete, and would win an Olympic bronze medal in the 800 metres in London the following year.

17.

Life around Emil can't ever have been boring, but it must also have been a trial at times. His insistence on turning everything into a 'performance' resulted in several misadventures in the weeks leading up to their marriage. His gold medal in London had been the first in athletics in the brief, thirty year history of Czechoslovakia at the Olympic Games. And with Dana being an Olympian too – she finished seventh in her international championship debut – their wedding was bound to be a huge occasion. They were home-grown heroes, both from Moravia, and they were to be married in Dana's home town of Uherské Hradiště, 'capital' of the area known as Slovácko, famous for its folklore festivals and wine production.

There was however a minor problem. Even though they had bought their wedding rings in London, Emil had still not asked Dana's parents for their permission. For once his bravado went missing, and after much prevarication one of Dana's friends had to mention casually in front of Dana's parents that they intended to get married. Even though he had voiced his concern, Dana's father probably realised that she would marry Emil whatever he said. The headstand he'd demanded as a proviso of marriage to his daughter was only accomplished with the help of Dana's friends. And Emil's precaution of ingratiating himself with mama Ingrová went awry with the burned cakes; following which she decided she'd be better off getting him to deliver some pies to various friends. Even that turned into another 'performance' with Emil trying to balance the tray on his head while jogging round the delivery circuit. Dana says that the neighbours' children brought back the pies that had bounced off the tray and fallen into the street.

Dana records the final travesty prior to the wedding. 'The high point of the wedding feast was supposed to be the pheasants. We went to get them the day before the wedding from the forest management in Velehrad. We could've gone by bus, but we took our bikes because everyone recommended that. We put the pheasants on our handlebars and we were coming home in a good mood. Of course Emil had to think up something different. He wanted us to hold each other's neck instead of the handlebars. It went quite well for a while. Then suddenly, a dog darted out of a ditch and jumped right in front of us. In a flash, we tumbled to the ground with the whole load. The dog started to tear the pheasants apart, and we had a hard job chasing it away'.

The couple may have seen it as fate when they discovered right at the beginning of their relationship that they were born on the same day of the same year, September 19, 1922, but when Agneška Zátopková found out on the morning of their marriage, she voiced concern, as Dana records in their co-autobiography, 'She was still shaking her head when she asked my mom what time I was born. When mom said immediately that I was born at 7am, Emil's mom's face brightened, and she said loudly so that everyone could hear, "Well, so Emil is older. He was born soon after midnight". That assured her that he was going to be the dominant one in our family and she was satisfied.

'Finally, after long preparations, tactical manoeuvres and much toing and froing, we finally got to the wedding itself. It was touch and go, because the people who lived further away started to come to Hradiště in the morning. The city radio also caused us another problem. I don't know if they did it by mistake, for fun, or out of past experience with army matters (they plan everything with a big time delay for the soldiers), but they announced the time of our wedding as two o'clock instead of four. As a result, there were that many spectators in the square, we almost couldn't get to the town hall. After the ceremony finished, the crowds delayed our wedding guests, such that they were arriving at the reception up to two hours late. Some lost their appetite completely'.

18.

Although I only spent a few hours at the Zátopek household in 1998, my first impression, backed up by talking to various friends of theirs convinced me that Dana and Emil were real pals. Both Lada Kořán and Štěpán Škorpil said that it was virtual 'open-house' in Troja, with people dropping round all the time, even via the nearby river Vltava, where friends would tie up their boats and stroll up the hill to visit. There didn't seem to be any of the sniping you get with some long-married couples, but that didn't stop them having a friendly 'dig' at each other from time to time. Shortly after I saw them, my friend Zane Branson went with a Serbian colleague to visit the couple. This was a period when Dana was substituting non-alcoholic beer for what she refers to elsewhere as, 'our national beverage'. With Emil chatting in another room, Dana served beer for Zane and Boban, giving them a glass of ersatz to take to Emil while swearing them to silence on its contents. According to Zane, Emil took the glass, winked and whispered to them, "Don't tell Dana, but she thinks I don't know that this is the non-alcoholic stuff".

In their co-autobiography, Dana extemporizes on the dangers of marriage, detailing the difficulties of coping with someone who was virtually institutionalised by dint of his having been, first in the Bata dormitories from the age of 14, then in army barracks for the rest of the time until they got married when they were 26. For example, Dana was initially confused that though Emil seemed to be wearing the same shirt every day, it never got dirty. Then she discovered that he was hiding the dirty shirt and secretly washing it himself, 'because he'd always done that'.

But that was the least of it. Emil, she quickly discovered was a tinkerer. There wasn't anything he didn't want to turn his hand to; and, for better or for worse, thought he could be good at. When they moved into their first apartment, a friend of Dana's, Majda took the spare room. The household quickly became a jousting-field between Emil and 'the girls,' as he referred to them. According to Dana, 'He didn't have the first idea about the advantages of being a married man. He didn't even want to hear about the traditional

51

Sunday dinner. He hated all of the things that he didn't get in the army. I often asked Majda for advice for something that would make Emil like my food, because she taught cooking at a college of nutrition…. We tried all kinds of food, meats fried, stewed and stuffed, but he always just took some bread and brought beer. Once we cooked a pot full of potatoes with kale for a change. When it was on the table, all of a sudden it seemed poor fare for a Sunday dinner, so we didn't even try to talk Emil into eating it. But as soon as he saw it on the plate, he said excitedly, Oh, girls, how happy you've made me right now! I love stuff like this the most!

'Our satisfaction faded a bit after the last sentence, but at least we understood him then. Beans, potatoes, peas, lentils, carrots that we didn't even have to cook for him, cabbage, spinach and all with a lot of onion, garlic or at least Romadur (cheese). All we had to do after that was to open the windows and Emil was glowing with satisfaction. That pleased him so much that he started to get interested in cooking. We were so happy about his interest that we completely overlooked the approaching danger. It started innocently enough. "You're cooking beans for me in this?" he asked. "Do you think I want to be poisoned?" And he continued with a scientific analysis, that vinegar in an aluminium pot creates aluminium acetate, which is good for swollen knees but not for his sporting body. Then he started in on lentils, sour cabbage and even ordinary cabbage - because that has its acids as well, he said. So we couldn't cook anything in the aluminium pots, which had been our main wedding gift.

'Similarly he said it was a crime to cut fruit with an ordinary knife because it destroys vitamins. We ended up under constant surveillance. His interest became an unpleasant rivalry. Not only did he learn how to cook his favourite meals perfectly, but he bragged about it so much in front of guests that it looked like no one else in the house could cook. He was making up new meals and new combinations and he was very precise about the recipes. We had to eat his meals all week long. He even gave us lectures about boiling water, making tea and decorating cakes. Sometimes I got mad but he just said that culinary evolution would never happen with conservative cooks such as myself.

'While we were trying to cope with this regime, he turned his attention towards beverages. The first era was a beer one. He refused to drink anything else. He said beer was healthy and it helped digestion. He wouldn't eat the dinner we prepared. He took a pitcher, ran to the pub, and just ate dry bread with the beer. The more we tried to talk him out of it, the more he resisted. Majda even tried to calculate how much alcohol he would drink in a year, but it was all in vain. So we chose another tactic. Once he came back with the full pitcher, we both handed him our glasses, asking for some. He poured the beer excitedly, believing that he had us converted. We didn't like the taste at first, but we got used to it. And we started to ask him for more so that there would be less for him. As a result, his excitement soon waned. When we sent him to a pub for ourselves, he started protesting, "You expect me to go to the pub just to get you beers?" Thus he lost his interest in our national beverage.'

Inevitably, running wasn't far from his thoughts, and Dana recounts a novel addition to his training schedule. 'He had an interesting idea for washing clothes. He ran hot water into the bath, poured Burnus (washing powder) into it, put his green shirts into it together with underwear, socks and sometimes even sweatpants. He then ran on it for half an hour, so vigorously that water was splashing all over the bathroom. Then he repeated the same with Persapon (liquid soap), and finally he did the same with clear water. While we were hanging up the clothes he wrote in his training diary, 'One hour skipping, at home'.'

He also helped with Dana's conditioning, building wall-bars at home so that she could do strengthening exercises, and erecting a trestle between trees in the garden at a height that the 1000 axe strokes per day he prescribed would mimic her throwing action. There was a degree of self-interest here, in that he didn't have to chop wood himself. But another initiative turned out to his serious disadvantage after a very short time. Dana recalls, 'At home, Emil continued to torture me. Every evening I had to do pull-ups and train my stomach muscles on the wall bars. Twice a week we would have a wrestling match. In the beginning, I flattened Emil after just a few minutes. But he began secretly going to the army wrestling club and observing different wrestling holds. He would then use these new techniques on me, so I no longer won quite as often as before. So as to not fall behind, I bought an instruction book for judo. One time we were fighting one another and I pinned him with his back against the boiling central heating. Three red stripes flared up instantly on his skin. It was not remotely intentional, it just happened as I got caught up in the moment. Nevertheless, Emil was very angry with me. From that point on, we decided we would only do basic wrestling without using any gimmicks'.

Dana goes on to detail a raft of pursuits that Emil would obsess over, some more successful than others. But like his father who had been a carpenter he was, apparently very good with his hands, and had a huge collection of tools. 'The best thing to do to stop his experiments was to give him some maintenance job,' Dana writes. That was his forte. When he had time, he could repair anything – leaking taps, broken switches, irons, sewing machines, and watches too. He made lampshades, shelves, and hangers for drying clothes. His masterpiece was a built-in wardrobe. There was barely a field he wouldn't plunge into. He had so many tools it would satisfy the most demanding craftsman'.

He eventually even helped to construct the family home in the suburb of Troja, near the city zoo, where the couple moved just before the Prague Spring. Although Štěpán Škorpil wasn't yet a personal friend, the journalist did know one of the neighbours, whereas the chief of the building work must have been one of the few people in Czechoslovakia who didn't know Zátopek. "My good friend, Jaroslav Škala," Škorpil told me, "said to the chief of building work, 'You don't know this man?' 'This is not a man,' the chief said, 'it is an animal. He is moving the materials around, quick, quick, quick, he never stops'. And Emil was 42, 43 at the time".

19.

I was fortunate in having two very good contacts in Prague, who would provide immeasurable help and occasional company during my several visits to the Czech Republic over two years of research. One was Carlo Capalbo, the Italian head of the Prague International Marathon, whose patrons were Dana and Emil. Carlo took me on my first visits to see Dana, and various of his staff gave regular help, contacting people and ferrying me to interviews, often long distances. The other was Zane Branson, a former top-class road and cross-country runner in the US college system, who had lived in Europe for two decades, and become a very successful athlete-manager with a stable of top East African runners. Zane had lived in Belgrade in Serbia for several years, but his friendship and shared projects with Capalbo, and the fact that the Czech Republic was in the Schengen area, and as such afforded his athletes easier travel throughout Europe meant that Zane kept a large apartment in Prague 7, close to the marathon offices. I had an open invitation to use Zane's flat whenever I was in Prague. There was the additional advantage that the flat was just a five minute jog from the parks of Letná and Stromovka, where Zátopek had trained and raced, even before he moved to Prague. And for post-run recreation, there were umpteen pubs and restaurants serving a wide variety of superb beer.

Zane had recommended the Café Spitfire, a mazy walk away from his flat. "It's got good beer, good music, not too loud, and it's relaxed". There was the inevitable caveat that smoking was permitted (Prague bars and restaurants were in the middle of a gradual transition to non-smoking). It was an old-fashioned place, an oblong room, with a high ceiling and a bar at one end near the door, and bench tables along the walls, with a couple of high round tables and stools near the bar. But the principal feature was the atmospheric, grainy monochrome blow-up reproductions of World War II Spitfires that covered the walls.

The place was so busy the first couple of times I went early evening that I never had occasion to ask the staff about either the name or the photos. But, barely a couple of days after my second visit there, while I was taking a late afternoon run around Letná, there came the unmistakeable racket of a Merlin engine. I stopped, and, sure enough, a 70 year old Spitfire clattered overhead, and continued across the Vltava, making a couple of passes over the city centre. My mystification festered for a couple of days more until, on a spare, sunny Sunday afternoon, I strolled up the street bordering Letná, to take a look inside the National Technological Museum. In pride of place, right in the centre of the Transport Section in the main hall on the ground floor, stood a WWII Spitfire. It all started to make sense. When the Nazis marched into Prague in 1939, many Czechoslovak airmen escaped to Poland and France, thence to Britain where, in mid-1940, the Inspectorate of the Czechoslovak Air Force was established. Its airmen, seconded initially to the RAF Volunteer Reserve, were based at RAF Cosford, near Wolverhampton, which just happens to be less than 25 kilometres from where I was born and raised. One of the hangars at Cosford was also the 'home' of UK indoor athletics for two decades, during which time I ran some of my best races there.

In July 1940, the first Czech RAF squadron, 310 was formed, and based at Duxford, now an air museum, close to Cambridge. Squadron 312 quickly followed, and both fought in the Battle of Britain. Including pilots in other RAF units, close to a hundred Czechoslovaks fought in the Battle, claiming close to 60 'kills'. Sgt Josef František, a Czech flying with a Polish squadron, 303, had 17 proven 'kills', the most of any Allied flyer in the Battle of Britain. Dana told me that one of her cousins was killed in the bombing of Hamburg; so he was probably in the bomber squadron, 311, that was subsequently formed. There was also another fighter squadron, 313, and in one guise or another over two thousand Czechoslovak airmen fought through to the end of the War. The first fighter squadron, 310 had a rather prosaic motto - 'We fight to rebuild'. But in keeping with the dashing image of airmen of any nation in war, the others chose brash, eg 312 went for Latin - 'Non multi sed multa' (Not many but much); 313 and 311 preferred the native lingo – 'Jeden jestřáb mnoho vran rozhání' (One hawk chases away many crows), and 'Vždy připraven' (Always ready). It turned out that the flyover I'd witnessed had been part of the celebrations for the unveiling of the Winged Lion monument at Klarov Park, in Prague's Old Town, honouring the 2,500 Czechoslovak men and women who served in the Royal Air Force in World War II. The Spitfire, a Mark XVIe, had been one of the last to be built, in 1945 at Castle Bromwich, around 30 kilometres from my birthplace.

Though Café Spitfire was only a few streets away from the Technological Museum, this still didn't explain the moody photos on the walls. The next time I went the bar was less busy, and a personable young woman behind the stoop explained that the owner was the grandson of the photographer, Ladislav Sitenský who had been a member of 312 squadron. But when his photographic talent was discovered he was immediately withdrawn from active service, and transferred to the Inspectorate in London, becoming squadron photographer and archivist. After the War, Sitenský had become one of Czechoslovakia's leading photographers, specialising in landscape. A few minutes later, Julia reappeared with a glossy book of monochrome reproductions, entitled simply *Sitenský*. As I was idling through the pages with mounting admiration, it occurred to me that Sitenský must have been a post-War contemporary of Zátopek, and since the book was far from being simply a collection of landscape photos, maybe there was a one of Emil? Sure enough, midway through the collection of full-page plates was the marvellous study reproduced on the cover of this book. Sitenský has captured the essence of Zátopek, the total involvement in his agony, oblivious to the camera, seeking only an issue in the gloam of a late summer evening in Strahov in 1955. He is past his best but, as usual, is giving his all.

On the facing page, there is a posed picture of a handsome young athlete (and journalist), Evžen Rošický, whose name is probably only remembered nowadays through the annual Memorial athletics meeting in Prague which bears his name. Rošicky and his father, Jaroslav had been members of an underground resistance group with the bravura name Captain Nemo. They were arrested in mid-1942, and executed by the Nazis one week later. When I mentioned the Sitenský photo-book, and the pictures of Zátopek and Rošický, to the veteran journalist, Štěpán Škorpil, he immediately shot back, "but Sitenský himself was also a good runner. He once finished second to Rošicky in the national championships 800 metres".

Sitenský's grandson, Václav, the bar owner later elaborated for me a story similar to the one about Zátopek's family being dead-set against him being a runner. "Ladislav's parents didn't want him to practise sport, because it would ruin his studies. They only found out about him running when he won a race and they read the report in the newspapers". I found an impeccable copy of the Sitenský book a day later, in one of the seductive warrens that are Prague's second hand bookshops. A week later, I met Sitenský's grandaughter, Václav's younger sister Adéla, who administers the Sitenský estate and photo-library. She gave me permission to use the picture in a blog to advertise the *BBC Radio 4* programme I made on Zátopek for the *Great Lives* series at the end of 2014.

And that wasn't the end of the coincidences. I was in the middle of booking one of my half dozen two-week trips to Prague throughout 2014, when an email pinged into my in-box. It was from the Czech Centre in London. The annual Czech arts festival, at the Institute for Contemporary Arts (ICA), was planning a showing of *Fair-Play* (original title in English) by the Paris-based Czech director, Andrea Sedlačková. There was to be a public debate after the ICA première and since the film was about young athletes being forced to take performance enhancing drugs during the Communist era, my cachet as an athletics writer throughout this period meant that I had been recommended to mediate the debate.

The connection was about as far off the wall as you could get. In 2010, I had been tangentially involved in the making of a documentary film about a Sahrawi runner, ostracised by the Moroccan occupiers of the Western Sahara, on the Atlantic coast of north-west Africa. I had visited the Sahrawi refugee camps in Western Algeria, to report on the situation, and interview the runner in question, Salah Ameidan. The producer of the documentary, *The Runner*, which won many prizes at film festivals across the world, had recommended me to the Czech Centre. This unlikely connection would prove invaluable, since on the evening of the *Fair-Play* première, I met Jiří Hošek, the Czech Radio representative in the UK, who lived just a few kilometres from me, in north-west London.

Over coffee a few days later, Hošek gave me a comprehensive personal view on recent Czech(oslovak) history, with particular reference to Zátopek and the peerless gymnast, Věra Čáslavská, whom I was eager to interview, since she, unlike Zátopek had never recanted her opposition to the Soviet invasion of their country. Even better, among other colleagues in Prague, Hošek gave me an introduction to Lubomir Šmatana who said he just happened to have a few documents which might interest me. Not half! A few thousand, as it turned out. Šmatana had acquired the microfiches of Emil Zátopek's secret police file, and duly sent them to me on my next visit to Prague.

20.

I mentioned right at the beginning that when I first visited the Zátopeks, their home showed no sign of being inhabited by athletics high achievers, Olympic gold medallists and multiple national champions. There wasn't a plaque, trophy or medal to be seen. Thirty years earlier, Emil had written, 'To be honest, I was never really serious about prizes. You can easily win a cross-country race in a city, where no one can touch you, and you get a prize so big you can barely carry it. On the other hand, you break a national record, and get one flag for the whole team. That's why I judge athletes, not by their trophies, but by their performances. I gave my own prizes away all the time, because I didn't know where to put them'.

The journalist and family friend, Štěpán Škorpil told me that, over their careers, Dana and Emil had won maybe fifty national titles. "She gave many things away, and she and Emil had lots of prizes. Back then, the limit on the prizes was 25 crowns, and there was one small statue that cost 24.99kr. And every time Dana and Emil won, they would get this small statue. Dana told me one time, we had FIFTY of these statues, 50 statues, all the same. So, every time somebody came for a coffee, when they left, Dana said, take a statue, please! And I asked, do you have one left, at least? No, not a single one".

Sometimes, there would be a more original prize, welcomed or not. One of the best stories in his consistently entertaining autobiography with Dana comes shortly after their marriage in late 1948. Maybe the censors were aware of his refined sense of humour, maybe not, and don't let me persuade you that this account is necessarily written with tongue firmly in cheek. 'Our cross-country championship took place in the old Czech town named Jičín back then. And on occasions like that, the locals want to show off. There was a solemn parade of the competitors with the town band playing, introduction of some of the local dignitaries, speeches about physical education and other subjects, mainly about the rich array of prizes. The main prize dominated them all: it was a huge painting of Trotsky in a wide golden frame. I barely had time to look at it before someone behind me quickly said, "That's our wedding gift for you and Dana. It's certain you'll win, none of the locals could possibly beat you!"

'I imagined how happy Dana would be if I brought the painting to our new home. With that in mind, I started running. We ran through a wide alley of linden trees, turned left and went around some gardens up a steep hill. I was running so fast I barely had time to notice the dark blue markers on the grass. At the top of the hill I was at least 200 metres ahead of the rest. Keep it up, I told myself, the painting is worth it. One young pioneer, probably a course marshal, was looking at the sky and enjoying the sunshine. He got a real fright when I flew past him. A few moments later, I heard someone calling and I thought, he's finally woken up, so he's at least encouraging the others. But his efforts are in vain, I thought, I've won this race already. The painting of Trotsky will be mine. I ran even faster down the hill, just to increase my lead.

'I was a bit surprised when I suddenly realised I couldn't see the blue markers anymore, but I guessed it wasn't necessary since I was on a straight path. I eventually came to a railway track – five roads, each leading to a different place – and the markers just weren't there. I thought to myself, that must have been the shouts I heard, for me! I turned around quickly and I ran back up the hill. Only to see all the runners turning left at the young pioneer. My huge lead had evaporated.

'When I re-joined the others, I was 29th. To make matters worse, it was in an area where I couldn't pass very easily. Some of the others were nice and friendly and got out of my way so that I could pass, others stupidly asked whether I was running the second lap already. There was no time for conversation. I saw more and more runners in front of me. I finally saw Zelenka from Gottwaldov (formerly Zlín) by the mill far ahead, and Novák from Liberec ahead of him. I got my head down, and gave it maximum effort, and I was going well. But we were back in Jičín already and I still wasn't in the lead. Novák was still 50 metres ahead, and being roared on by the locals, and by all the cross-country fans too. They were all shaking their heads when they saw me, "Look, Zátopek can't keep up with him. See how exhausted he looks - a total mess!" Fortunately, there was still a three kilometre stretch around the cemetery before the finish. I can't get lost in there, I thought, and in fact I killed off Novák so decisively that I had to wait for him for an entire minute at the finish. I was tired, but I got my 'Trotsky' in the end.'

21.

Despite his various new pastimes – cooking, brewing, painting, repairing, inventing, even wrestling - married life was not so distracting that Zátopek did not find time to break two world records in 1949. Both came in Ostrava, barely 30 kilometres from his birthplace in northern Moravia, and close to the Silesian coalfields and the border with Poland. The first record came at a military championship in mid-June at the suburban stadium of Vítkovice, and since he hadn't had time for lunch, Zátopek records that he took some bread and boiled eggs, and stopped off for a beer, another indication of just how much 'liquid bread' is part of the national diet. In the co-autobiography, he expresses surprise at how well the stadium announcer had prepared for his race, since when he immediately ran away from the rest of the field, there began a running commentary on how close or far ahead he would be from the then world record holder, Vilho Heino of Finland, whom he had killed off so easily in the Olympic Games the previous year.

'To my surprise, people liked it a lot. They clapped after every announcement and after the fifth kilometre they started to cheer loudly. After the split time for the sixth kilometre was announced some boys came to trackside and started to chant, "We...Want... A... Record". I knew it wouldn't be that easy, but I decided that if the seventh kilometre made a record look likely, I would try to keep up the pace till the very end. Now I was listening myself for the commentator to call the time. And really, he announced I was running faster than Heino during his best performance. So I really dug in and I fought the fatigue and the stop-watch through the final three kilometres. On the last lap, all the spectators were on their feet and I ran through the tape to clamour and confusion from the terraces. All three stop watches recorded the new world record - 29min 28.2sec. I'd beaten Heino's record by seven seconds'.

He had also lapped the second man twice, and beaten him by close to three minutes, so rather like the preparatory beer we are a long way from the modern elite athlete's idea of attacking a world record with one if not more pacemakers. Another critical difference is that this was just one of *eleven* 10,000 metres races that Zátopek ran between mid-June and mid-October that season, four of them in Ostrava alone. But there was symmetry; his first 10,000 of the season had been a world record, and when Heino shocked him and everyone else by retrieving the world record shortly afterwards at 37 years of age, Zátopek went back to Ostrava for the final 10,000 of the season.

If the stadium announcer had prepared well for Zátopek's first world record in Ostrava, everyone got in on the act for the second one. The local paper, *The Worker* produced a special edition with the headline, ZÁTOPEK ATTACKS WORLD RECORD, and the organisers even brought his parents from Kopřivnice. As the man himself wrote, 'Since everything had been so meticulously prepared, I warmed up carefully, so as not to mess anything up and disappoint everyone. I prepared my 'splits' (lap times) for a finishing time of 29.22 and after 25 laps the timekeepers stopped the watches at 29min 21.2sec. Hooray! A new world record! People could read about it in the newspapers immediately and they couldn't get over their surprise. They even introduced my parents to the spectators. While mom was accepting compliments, dad outdid himself and even said into the microphone, "Go Sports".'

22.

For any Czech or Slovak over the age of 50, the name of Jáchymov has a resonance approaching that of Auschwitz, Belsen or Dachau. Unlike the Nazi concentration camps, the Czechoslovak Communist authorities did not set out to exterminate all of their captives, just some of them. But it was only a matter of degree. For those who died, for those who survived, and for those who remain intent on remembering, there was good cause to refer to the 'Jáchymov Inferno' or 'Jáchymov Hell'; and the nearby 'Tower of Death'. Yet Jáchymov or Joachimsthal in the German rendering is a centuries old town whose activities have had an otherwise huge impact on world culture.

It was there that Marie Curie-Skłodowska gathered the pitchblende from which she would isolate radium, the most important stage on her journey to one of two Nobel prizes. And three centuries earlier, the silver mines had lent themselves to minting of the highest quality coins, one of which was called the Joachimsthaler or 'thaler' a word which would eventually transmute into 'dollar'. A by-product of the late nineteenth century uranium mines was radon, minimally-laced radium water, which was used to create the first radon spa in the then Joachimsthal in 1906. The town in the Ore Mountains took its place alongside the great central European spa towns of Karlsbad, now Karlovy Vary, Franzenbad and Marienbad.

Since the demise of Communism, Jáchymov has been edging back to its former spa-town glory. And when I went to stay in mid-June, 2015, it was in the opulent surroundings of the original spa hotel, the splendidly named Radium Palace. The clientele was, inevitably older, with Czechs, Slovaks, Germans, a few Brits and Americans and, signposting the location of 'new money', plenty of Russians and Gulf Arabs. With an introduction from one of the Prague Marathon staff, who went there every summer for radium bath treatment for her rheumatism, and having mentioned the magic word 'Zátopek', the hotel staff could not have been more accommodating. I got a complimentary radium bath, which may or may not have eased the semi-permanent stiffness in the legs of the ageing long-distance runner; and they also supplied an interpreter both for my visit to the nearby mines, and the following day, for a conversation with a former worker who had actually known Zátopek when the latter was working there in the early 1970s, during his labouring exile.

The uranium and silver have long been mined out, and the two remaining mines in central Jáchymov serve only to pump lightly radiated water to the several spa hotels at the bottom, ie posh end of town. Once a week, on a Wednesday afternoon, there is a conducted visit, mostly for spa hotel guests, to the mines. After a cautionary introduction from the mine foreman, a dozen of us togged up in helmets with lamps, and overalls, and crammed, six at a time, into a rackety elevator which dropped us 500 metres or so in two and a half minutes to the 12th floor of the Svarnost (Concord) mine. We spent about three hours traipsing round the corridors and old workings (including a cave chapel, complete with plastic patron saint and electric candle), of the Svarnost and Josef mines, with water dripping from the ceilings and running alongside the worn duckboards which kept our feet relatively dry.

These pits were where the dozen members of the world champion ice hockey team had been sent to dig uranium in the early fifties, at the same time as Lada Kořán, an early training partner of Zátopek, and one of my principal interviewees. Kořán had had a colourful life, as I detail elsewhere, but the lowlight of it was the eighteen years that he spent at Jáchymov following his arrest while trying to smuggle his wife and young child across the German border (ironically, not far from Jáchymov), in 1950.

"The guy who was leading me through the borderline was killed, three feet to my left," Kořán told me in mid-2015. "It was tragic. It was something I was not born for. I was a peaceful guy, good with people around me, and now this was happening to me. They got me to the StB (secret) police station. They beat me up, accused me of espionage and high treason, and sentenced me to eighteen years of hard labour. Ten years, I was a miner in a uranium mine in Jáchymov. And I can tell you that athletics, running, the hard training saved my life. The work there, it did not hit me the way it hit people who had not trained like me. I believe it saved my life.

"(Milada) Horáková was a colleague. We were in jail at the same time. Ten of the ice-hockey team, world champions from 1947, they were there. Lots of

RAF men were in Jáchymov, even generals. It was unheard of, incredible paranoia. But jail at that time was such a tragic hard time for everybody who was there. I was disciplined, I was not smoking, I was just trying to be (to live), and I was fighting for my life every day. When I came home after ten years in the concentration camp, there was no job for me anywhere, because they wanted me to make bricks for 600 crowns a month. That was nothing to live on. I had a wife and son, so I went back to Jáchymov as an electrician/ technician, and they wanted my services, and I was making money then, in the same outfit as when I was a prisoner. Jáchymov was under the hand of Moscow, it was a republic within a republic. There you were under the 'protection' of these bastards. I was there for eight years, but then it came the Prague Spring, and we thought we would already be somewhere else, and not in the Soviet sphere. So I was doing my best to get out, and I did".

23.

A few kilometres south of Jáchymov, near the town of Ostrov, we stopped off at the now abandoned site of the infamous 'Tower of Death,' sometimes referred to as the Red Tower, due to the red brick buildings. During the early 1950s, the uranium ore extracted in Jáchymov and elsewhere was transported here, and sorted by hand by a variety of political prisoners, dissidents, and Jehova's Witnesses, none of whom was wearing any sort of protective gear. Inevitably scores, if not hundreds died from radiation or illnesses brought on by their weakened state.

A mini-railway (one of its engines is on public display near the Radium Palace in Jáchymov itself) brought the ore from the trucks to a bay close by, where it was loaded onto a conveyor which took it to the top of the Tower. A system of sieves sorted the valuable ore from the grit and dust which filled the air inside the four floors of the tower, where the prisoners worked. Most of the overseers were Russian, since the crushed ore was transported in its entirety to the Soviet Union, to feed their nuclear programme. The site was later taken over by the Škoda vehicle company, and trolley buses were produced there until that closed in 2004. Four years later, the company donated the site to the Confederation of Political Prisoners, and it was declared a National Heritage site, though not yet developed and opened to the public.

One of the prisoners working at the Death Tower (and Jáchymov) during the worst period was Jan Haluza, Zátopek's early and only coach. Dr Haluza, as he was styled (a legal honorific) was a real survivor. Despite the depredations of the Death Tower, and the other privations and beatings he suffered, Haluza lived until he was 97, dying in mid-2011, over a decade after his star pupil. Following the Velvet Revolution, when they both re-appeared fully in Czechoslovak society, after their effective internal exile, Zátopek was famously quoted as saying, "Without Haluza, there would have been no Zátopek". Though both men admitted that Haluza's 'coaching' was fairly minimal, little more than pointing the newcomer, some eight years younger, in the right direction, it is nonetheless fortuitous that Haluza, then the best middle and long distance runner in Czechoslovakia lived in Zlín and, almost inevitably worked at the same Bata factory.

Haluza was a multiple national champion, at cross country and steeplechase on the track, and would go on to twice win the oldest and most famous road race in Czechoslovakia, the Běchovice to Prague 10k, founded in 1897, and unlike the far more celebrated Boston Marathon, inaugurated the same year, it has been contested without a break since then. The 2016 edition marks its 120th running. Curiously, Zátopek never ran this race until long after he retired, finally trotting round in the mid-1960s when, according to recent biographer and political historian, Pavel Kosatík, he didn't even win his age group.

Over twenty years earlier, when Zátopek resumed his nascent running career in spring 1942, one of his new acquaintances from the *Run Through Zlín* asked him to make up a team that was going to Brno, now the Czech second city. 'They needed me for two races, the 1500m and 3000m,' writes Zátopek in *As Told by Dana and Emil*. 'To my surprise, I won them both. I was even more surprised when someone came and said that Dr Haluza was at the track, and wanted to talk to me. He was our best long-distance runner at that time, double winner of Běchovice. I'd never had the courage to even say hello to him, that´s how much I respected a famous sportsman back then. But he just said that I ran well, and invited me to come and train with him at the stadium the next day. Of course I couldn't wait. My winter melancholy, when I'd said goodbye to running, was long gone.'

In the typically downbeat style which permeates his contributions to his and Dana's co-autobiography, Emil records those first trips to the local stadium. 'It was a wonderful experience to run in the stadium where all the champions of that time trained. Aside from Dr Haluza I also saw up close his biggest rival, Tomáš Šalé ..... We began by running about two kilometres. Then we bent forwards and back, and farted loudly, as if we were competing in that. Then we ran again, and did some bounding on the other side of the stadium with different styles. There we leaned against the fence and shook our legs to all different sides so much I got a neck-ache from it. When we sprinted the straights and jogged the bends, I was totally exhausted. Then they told me that was just a warm-up, and the real training was to come. So I just watched that time.

'When Šalé ran his fast two-hundreds, Dr Haluza told me, 'See, that's what made him a champion. Remember, speed is the basis of athletics'. That stayed in my mind. When he wanted me to run 300 metres at the next training session, I ran like a scared mouse. I was wondering how long it took me to run it, but he just told me I should run it again five minutes later. I guess it's supposed to be that way, I said to myself and I was looking forward to my first race. I ran a three kilometres with Dr Haluza and I led for the first half of the race. I finished behind him in 9min 12sec. The Zlín newspapers wrote, 'Wonderful achievement by Zátopek at 3000m'. I didn't 'know the ropes' in distance running, but I liked the headline. I was reading that article the whole day, and in the evening, I was back at the stadium. Not long after that I ran 1500m in 4min 12sec; and I was in the newspapers again. They started to notice me in our club. They called me 'The Badger' thanks to my dishevelled hair, and they let me go even to the most important races.

'I definitely showed a performance there with which I could win many races, but not, it seemed, in Zlín. The best runners there were Dr. Haluza and Šalé. Whenever I raced with one or the other, try as hard as I could, I always ended up second. The boys laughed at me and asked me why I was racing at all, since I never won anything. What was there to do other than making up stories about health and fitness. Waiting for those phenomenons to get old or even die out would be waiting in vain. I slowly got used to being called Emil the Second.'

In an interview in *Katolický týdeník* (Catholic Weekly) in August 2008, Haluza gave his own perspective. 'To begin with, Emil really did not have an appetite for competition. He saw his future in a chemical lab. But I soon managed to awaken a fighting spirit within him. As soon as he finished work, which was a demanding job, he would come straight to the running track. It was a pleasure to work with him. He never lost his optimism and was cheerful and sincere. But lack of food was a serious problem. I often felt sorry for the kid when, exhausted, he would ask for just a piece of bread. I couldn't give him anything – everything was rationed. At least work was able to provide him with track shoes so that he didn't have to destroy his legs like I did by running in plimsolls.

'Being a trainer meant something different back then than it does today.

Money didn't play a role, rather it was a relationship based on friendship. During training I didn't force Emil to do anything or dictate anything to him, we simply ran together, two friends on the track. I was about eight years older and considerably more experienced than Emil so I simply advised him and tried to help him refine his running style. We gradually made progress. He picked his legs up more, lengthened his strides and developed his breathing technique. Emil welcomed all advice, no matter how small, with enthusiasm. He was always asking questions and he also tried to think up improvements for himself.

'I used to say jokingly that Emil is a grateful student, but an ungrateful athlete. For a long time I motivated him by telling him that if he ever wanted to beat me, he would have to work like a horse. Then, in 1944, it happened. To begin with, he used to always take second place just behind me. Then, it was in September, he suddenly had three victories in a row and at the same time achieved national records in the 2000, 3000, and 5000 metres. I was the first person to congratulate him. Then the battlefront drew near and all the factories were closed for good. In the summer of 1945 when sport could take off once again, I felt that my time had come to an end. I was over 30 and I wanted to focus on my work and my wife. Emil (then) created his own extraordinarily good method. He no longer wanted a trainer, nor did he need one. He joined the army, moved to Prague and just got better and better. I followed his success with delight, especially his Olympic triumph in London in July 1948..... It was a shame that I could only watch his most famous 'Helsinki moment' through prison bars.'

There were times during my research in Prague and elsewhere when I got the strong impression that everybody knew everybody else in Czechoslovakia, so frequent and many were the connections I encountered between people and places. But, I suppose it's a function of a smaller society numerically, with a correspondingly smaller nucleus of athletes and a tighter nexus of elites, whatever their political leaning. So, it came as no surprise to learn that when Haluza, a committed Christian was arrested on trumped up charges in early 1948, there was even an unsuccessful attempt to link him to the equally ill-founded 'treason' case which eventually led two years later to the execution of Milada Horáková (I will expand on this disgraceful case later). In the same interview in 2008, Haluza recalled, 'By the end of 1945 I was chair of the Regional Committee of the People's Party (Christian & Democratic Union) youth group in Zlín. We used all our free time to focus our efforts on beating the Communists in the upcoming elections. We succeeded in our region, but unfortunately not in the entire country.

'And my comrades did not forgive me. At first they attempted to woo me over to their side. They offered leading roles in the Bata Company in exchange for joining the Party; they offered a reward for opposition. I categorically refused. Shortly after, in 1948, I was arrested. I became a member of the so-called 'anti-state, subversive Zlín group', one of the first groups in the country falsely accused. Attempting to violently overthrow the regime, they claimed. I stress now, just as I did back then, that all of the accusations were fabricated. Yes, we strived for freedom and democracy, but always through peaceful means in accordance with the law and God's Ten Commandments. The arrest of my wife was meant to force me to confess and accuse other people. They were never able to force me to do anything. I was brought up with strict discipline and sport toughened me up too. My education in law helped as well. When I realised that cowardly lawyers were not helping their own clients, in fact sometimes they were even aggravating them, I decided to defend myself. Perhaps this saved several years of my life but I still left the court with six years hard labour. After nine months in custody, my wife was eventually freed. Of course, until my release, she was forced to live in a constant state of fear, humiliation and was always under observation.

'I thought that after being tortured I already had the worst behind me, but I was deeply mistaken. After a while they secretly decided to involve me in the Milada Horáková case. The secret police in Uherské Hradiště (Dana's home town) were apparently trying to get extra credit. For many long months, during interrogations I underwent cruel, inhumane beatings, which alternated with psychological terror. Once, the sole of my foot was beaten to a bloody pulp and I was submitted many times to beastly torture by electric shock. The sadism of the interrogators was indescribable. Fortunately they were unable to break me; the disgraceful trial involving Milada Horáková and the others had to start without me. I consider it a miracle that I so clearly managed to save my own life.'

The striking quality about Haluza, in common with Lada Kořán and others who suffered imprisonment and torture during this period while Zátopek was being fêted across the country and throughout the world, is that none of them nurtured any rancour towards him, or even expressed any criticism for his inability to help them. On the other hand, many younger people, those born immediately before, or after the Velvet Revolution were much more critical of Zátopek. One thirty something journalist at Czech Radio, told me, "I sympathised, but I did not cry for him". 'What would hatred achieve,' said Haluza in the *Katolický týdeník* interview in 2008. 'I didn't even feel any joy when the judge who had sent me to prison committed suicide. As for Zátopek, I think that he and his wife Dana had already demonstrated enough courage by regularly keeping in touch with me after my release (in 1954)'.

Kořán was similarly unequivocal in his support for Zátopek, pointing out that the celebrity had his own, substantial problems with the Communist authorities. Kořán spent over a decade in Jachýmov as a prisoner, and even went back to work there, but after his release he spent some time living near Prague, and decided to go to watch an international rowing event on the Vltava. During our interview in early 2015, opposite the Vltava, in Porus restaurant, where he had spent so many lively hours with Zátopek immediately after the War, he told me, "Emil was there, I saw him. He was everywhere, he was a very social guy. Somehow he saw me, and he jumped down from the lorry, and ran 50 metres or so to me, and embraced me, and said, 'Lada, this is so beautiful to see you. We thought you were dead'. That, I thought was heroic, because the place was full of StB (secret police) agents. They saw everything he was doing, because they were on him, they had to report every day what he was doing, who he was talking to. We had five or ten minutes together, then he had to go because the race started. But in the next few days, weeks, months, I saw what was happening to him. They were watching everybody who had anything to do with the west".

Kořán was even forgiving about his friend's renunciation of the *2000 Words Manifesto*, saying, "Some people were disappointed with him. Me, because I was in the concentration camp, and know that he could have gotten in the concentration camp because of this stupidity… it was not stupidity, it was heroism to do something like that… He suffered terribly…working with all these simple people (in exile). I know personally what it means, because one project I did, for the construction company, living in the caravans like an idiot, like a pig, and you have to have your eyes and ears open (and say), 'they will not break me'. He had so many of them around him, and they didn't know anything but (to) do their job. And drink and play cards inside the maringotka (caravan). It's very difficult to stay sane, but he did, for himself, but unfortunately he started to drink".

24.

Apart from a minor blip in the middle of 1951, when military duties intervened, the four seasons from 1950, the year when he went undefeated and won the European 5000/10,000 metres double, through the Olympic treble of 1952, on to the middle of 1954, when he surprised even himself by setting two world records inside a week, were the halcyon days of Zátopek's career. But typically he could not rack up these accomplishments without drama of some sort. TV journalist Štěpán Škorpil was not the only one of my interviewees to describe Emil as an 'actor' and wherever he went, the setting, whether street or stadium was a stage for the leading performer of his, or perhaps, any (athletic) age. And by this time, he was the most famous Czechoslovak in the world. In his obituary in the *Prague Post* in late 2000, Czech Olympic Committee member, Jiři Vicha recalled that during his own travels back then, 'Many times, people thought our President was Tito (of Yugoslavia), but everyone knew who Zátopek was'.

This view was corroborated from an unlikely source, the British comedian Alexei Sayle. Son of a Liverpool Marxist, as a special treat his parents took him on holiday to Czechoslovakia in the late 1950s. In one of his biographical works, *Stalin Ate My Trousers*, published in 2011, Sayle records, 'The most famous, indeed the only famous Czech at the time was the athlete Emil Zátopek, also known as the 'Flying Czech' because he was so fast or 'Emil the Terrible' due to his ugly running style.... We were already aware of Zátopek, who was particularly admired in our house because in the 5000 metres at Helsinki he had beaten a great British hero, Christopher Chataway. Chataway, an ex-Public schoolboy and a bit of a Young Tory was second, but after being overtaken by Zátopek, he tripped and fell. We especially liked that'. Despite being sketchy on the details – Chataway was in fact fifth, and Sayle overlooks that Zátopek won the marathon in Helsinki too – you get the drift.

If Zátopek needed any re-enthusing for a new season, the 10,000 metres world record at the end of 1949 did that, and he records that he was never better prepared for a campaign than in 1950. Though this was probably the period of maximum paranoia at home, with the Communists preparing the show-trials of Milada Horáková and her 'accomplices' and of the members of the world champion ice-hockey team, Dana and Emil were enjoying the benefits of their celebrity which included what was becoming increasingly rare for their beleaguered compatriots, international travel. The couple was invited to train with Soviet athletes at the Black Sea resort of Sochi.

'You can look at the snowy Kavkaz peaks with one eye,' wrote Emil, 'and with the other see the crystal-clear waters of the Black Sea, sparkling in the hot southern sun. In Moscow there were still traces of snow, but in Sochi, the palms were in bloom. We included some sea-swimming into our training schedule, although we had to share the water with some playful dolphins. I once wanted to pet one of them, and I swam so far that I could hardly get back'.

The immediate result was that he set another 10,000 metres world record, this time putting it way beyond the reach of former holder, Vilho Heino. And for maximum effect, he did it in the then HQ of long-distance running – Heino's home country, Finland. Even better, he did it at the totemic track at Turku, the birthplace of his illustrious predecessor, Paavo Nurmi. Nowadays, the stadium is named after Nurmi, and he is celebrated every midsummer with the Paavo Nurmi Games and the Paavo Nurmi Marathon. Emil had set a national record for 5000 metres, 14min 06sec in Helsinki just beforehand, and wrote, 'Two days later I got even bigger ovations in Turku. I improved the 10,000 metres world record by 19 seconds, which I didn't expect myself. The Finns who especially understand the long distances stayed and applauded me long after I had finished the race. I also fell in love with them. They could appreciate my performances even though I had taken the world record from their best runner'.

But the focus of the season was the European Championships in Brussels. After Turku, the 10,000 metres title was even more a foregone conclusion for our hero. But the highlight, already being eagerly anticipated, was the re-match between home-boy Gaston Reiff, who had not only prevailed against Zátopek's grandstand finish in the mud-spattered 5000 metres at the Olympic Games in London in 1948, but had also had the temerity to stray into Emil's territory, the Strahov stadium in Prague in mid-1949, and beat him again at 5000 metres. And on that occasion the gap was far more than a metre, Reiff had won handsomely. The stage was set for the next showdown. But one of the principal actors nearly didn't make it.

'I didn't have to worry about my form after my successes in Finland,' wrote Emil. 'I just shouldn't have eaten any meat. I'm not that into meat, but when Dana brought me a roast duck from Moravia, I accepted her words like a dutiful husband - "Take this so you're not hungry". She saved me the last piece and I felt I could smell something a little bit. But I ate it anyway, and drank a litre of milk and ate few pears with it. I had an appointment at the dentist shortly afterwards; and it came just in time. When it was my turn, I fainted and instead of the dentist's chair I ended up in a hospital ward with acute food-poisoning. It was almost an athletic tragedy – to get sick on Friday when I had to run the 10,000 metres in Brussels the following Wednesday. But it happened - vomiting, diarrhoea, high fevers. I lost five kilos in a single day. When Dana saw me, she started to cry, "Why did you eat it?" "Because you gave it to me! Don't cry and bring me some sweatpants for training. We're flying on Tuesday".

'The doctors ordered me to stay in bed and didn't want to hear a thing about the European Championships. They wouldn't even give me anything to eat. But I was lucky that the next day was Saturday. The doctors left and there were only the nurses in the hospital. They too only gave me bitter tea without food, but there was an excellent canteen in the basement. I ate two sausages, a lot of mustard, some bread and beer (again!) and I went behind the buildings to train. On Saturday I felt light-headed and very weak. On Sunday I was running around the buildings so well that all the nurses were watching me from the windows. "Imagine that!" they were telling the other patients. "It's a miracle - not eating ànything, just drinking that tea, and running like that". In the end, even the doctors had to admit that I wasn't doing so badly. They finally let me out on Tuesday, and I went straight to Brussels. The following day I won the 10,000 metres by a whole lap from Mimoun.'

'THE BIG FACE-OFF: REIFF – ZÁTOPEK' roared the Brussels' dailies. Like many such events, the race did not quite live up to the hyperbole. As in the London Olympics - not forgetting the demise of the marathoner Gailly, who had been leading until the threshold of Wembley - Reiff was the Belgians' only hope for a gold medal. And Reiff's coach, Marcel Alavoine was going to do all he could to convince Zátopek that he could not win. Prior to the race he said, "Gaston will win, there's nothing you can do". And as the athletes lined up for the start, Alavoine yelled at Emil, "Gaston will win in 14.03". 'The race was really fast,' wrote Zátopek. 'It took me two laps to get ahead, but then, sooner than in London, Reiff suddenly took over. The 60,000 Belgians began shouting as one man, "Ga – ston, Ga – ston, Ga – ston!" I had to work really hard to keep up, so that he wouldn't get a lead of more than 10 or 15 metres, which I knew I could make up at the finish. And that's just what happened. In fact, I was getting closer with each lap, until I passed him about 700 metres from the finish. I don't think he expected that because when he looked back, he seemed really scared. "You've done your best, haven't you?" I thought to myself.

'When the bell announced the last lap, I ran so fast that there was space between us within just five metres. Suddenly the whole stadium fell silent, except for the place where I knew my team was sitting. I heard, "Emiiiiiiiil!" In that final lap, I took 130 metres out of him. The whole finishing straight was empty in front and behind, until Reiff finally appeared there. When Mimoun realized he was struggling, he sprinted hard and 'got' him at the line, by a vest. To add to the achievement, I ran a national record of 14min 03sec, which was exactly the time that Reiff's coach had said he would do. Good for him, I thought, he shouldn't have messed with me.'

25.

According to Zátopek, the initial suggestion that he should run the marathon as well as the 5000 and 10,000 metres in Helsinki, leading to that unprecedented historic hat-trick of Olympic distance golds, came from one of his army bosses the previous year. Yet his 1951 campaign had the most inauspicious start of any season in his career. And to us also-rans, it's gratifying to learn that even a multiple world record holder and Olympic champion like Zátopek runs badly if he doesn't train. As he later wrote, 'I was working at the ministry back then, and I was in the office from early morning to late evening and I didn't have much time left to train. I was running so poorly that 15 minutes for 5000 metres was almost a peak performance. Our best miler, Vašek Čevona even beat me in a 3000. In our country that was an occasion that not only woke the spectators up, but also the journalists – that's how the Minister of Defence found out. Čevona was a civilian, and as you can guess, the army is very careful to have its people do better than civilians. The Minister decided that my job in the office should be done by somebody who was no good at sport, and that I should go back to representing the army. The team leader welcomed me with a very pleasant offer, "Look, comrade captain, we have to look at this from a Bolshevik perspective. You have my full support, and now all you need to do is run and run and run, so that you get back to top form".'

It only took a few weeks before Zátopek was taking close to a minute off those sedate season openers. In August 1951, he won the 5000 metres at the Festival of Sport in Berlin in 14min 11sec. Speculation was already turning to the Olympic Games the next year. 'A lot of people were saying, "So, Emil, it's going to be two gold medals in Helsinki, not just one like in London, right?" But Lieutenant-Colonel Sábl had a more interesting idea, "You know, the nicest solution would be to enter all three long distance events, and win them all. What's a marathon for you since you're running 30 km a day anyway?" '

Thus, running the marathon, his first, in Helsinki 1952 was far from a whim or a last minute decision. A year before the Olympic Games, he decided to test himself by running his longest track event thus far, the 20,000 metres, which is often paired with the one hour run (for distance). For good measure, since this was Zátopek, he ran the event(s) twice in two weeks. One was an obligatory appearance at the Army Championships, for which he could choose the distance, so he decided to go for the Czechoslovak records in the first one, in Strahov Stadium, Prague on September 15. So easy did it prove that he knocked over a minute off Vilho Heino's world record for 20,000 metres, with 61min 15.8sec, recording 19,558 metres at the hour, 200 metres better than Heino en route. He was ecstatic. 'It was a wonderful result. I achieved my objective, and I wasn't even out of breath afterwards. A world record was never so easy. I'd discovered that races above 10 km were easier for me than the ones under. I didn't even need to go to Houšťka anymore. But I'd reproach myself if I didn't, because why shouldn't I attempt to run full tilt right from the start?'

Which is what he did, on September 29 in the tiny Houšťka stadium in the middle of the forest near Stará Boleslav, where he was rewarded with not only two more world records, but totemic ones, with the first sub-one hour 20,000 metres in history – 59min 51.8sec – and the first 20k plus one hour run – 20,052 metres. 'And as a rehearsal for a marathon it was truly wonderful,' he wrote. 'I would pack my suitcase and go to the Olympics right away if I could. But there were still nine months 'til Helsinki and anything could happen in the interim'.

And, inevitably, it did.

26.

The start of Olympic season 1952 was as ominous as the events leading up to the European Championships two years earlier, when he had found himself in hospital less than a week before Brussels. At least on this occasion, when he got tonsillitis and a high fever which confined him to bed in springtime, he had two months to recuperate. Nevertheless, now having the Olympic marathon in mind, and having confessed that he did better at events over 10,000 metres, he began to have doubts as to whether he would even compete in the 5000 metres in Helsinki, a race which he later described as the most eagerly awaited of the whole Games. And with reason. While he was struggling to regain form, going from 14min 47sec at the end of May to 14min 22sec by mid-June, he had still been well beaten in the latter by two Soviet runners, Vladimir Kazantsev and Nikifor Popov. Meanwhile one of his principal rivals, Herbert Schade of West Germany was running 14min 06.6sec in Nienburg. According to his autobiography with Dana, he decided that he would forego the Olympic 5000 metres if he couldn't break 14min 20sec in the national championships in late June, exactly a month prior to the same distance in Helsinki. He ran 14min 17.6sec.

But first the defence of his Olympic title from London. The 'Czech Locomotive' nickname had already been circulating at home for at least two years, but the 'Human Locomotive' gained wider currency following his 10,000 metres victory on the opening day of the Olympic Games in Helsinki, July 20, 1952. After a couple of laps of sparring, he went to the front and strung out the field, so that they were running in Indian file behind. The next morning, a cartoon in one of the Finnish newspapers portrayed him as the engine, blowing off steam, followed by a long string of carriages, Mimoun with a French beret, the Russian Anufriev with a Soviet flag, the British runners, Gordon Pirie and Frank Sando sporting Union Jacks. Off the page, only Mimoun stayed with him for any length of time, but the Algerian-born Frenchman was dropped well before the end, and finished over 100 metres behind as Zátopek won in an Olympic record time of 29min 17sec.

The 5000 metres however was, as widely forecast a vastly different proposition. But the result would vindicate the debates that Zátopek had had with team coaches earlier in the season; coaches who believed that he should modify his training to do faster repetitions, in order to deal with the likes of Schade and other emerging talents, such as Britain's Chris Chataway. The 5000 metres heats, two days after the 10,000 metres final only heightened the anticipation. Mimoun won the first heat in a French record time of 14min 19.0sec. Schade set an Olympic record of 14min 15.4sec in the second heat, and when five men broke away in the final heat, the polyglot Zátopek pointed out to the others that since it was five to qualify for the final, they needn't kill themselves over the final laps. Nevertheless, Aleksandr Anufriev kept up the pace, so Zátopek gestured for him to carry on, and when he himself approached the finish line, he ushered Bertil Albertsson of Sweden ahead, and contented himself with a relaxed third place finish which, for the statistically minded was his only 'defeat' in a dozen races over the years in the land of the once kings of distance.

Zátopek described the final, another two days later, as his best ever race. And that is the self-confessed testament of a competitor, because this was not a runaway, as so many of his career successes had been, but a race between peers with the lead swapping several times over the fourteen minutes of the event, and the result in doubt until the final straight. Defending champion Reiff was prominent early on, but eventually dropped out, and the principal protagonists over the crucial final kilometre devolved into Zátopek, his shadow Mimoun, the marginal pre-race favourite Schade, and the youngster Chataway. The game of musical chairs became even more frantic as they hit the bell with Schade taking the lead again.

For the last three decades, if not longer, it has become commonplace for 5000 and 10,000 metres medallists to run the last lap at sub-60sec pace. It was not the case in Zátopek's day, and I would venture that his successors learned from and then refined his training in order to achieve this. But in Helsinki, he knew that his adversaries had begun their sprint too early. Talking in the early 1990s to Rich Benyo, editor of the US magazine, *Marathon & Beyond*, he even said, 'To be too fast is dangerous. My basic speed was low. I was not talented for sprinting. But I did very much work-out in training, fast and slow, fast and slow, but non-stop, and my record was very good, my recovery was extreme. I was used to running forty times 400 metres, no problem. But runners are not used to sprinting 400 metres at the end of 5000 metres. As I started to sprint, Chataway, Schade and Mimoun started sprinting again, of course without recovery. For me, it was not dangerous, but my adversaries, after 200 metres, they were tired, they could not accelerate more'.

In his co-autobiography, Zátopek details the final 400 metres, 'I was fourth again, behind Schade, Mimoun and Chataway. It was a very unpleasant surprise for me, to be caught in the finish that I'd been preparing so diligently for four years. But I chased and felt them slowing down with 200 metres to go. "I see, you´re done already," I thought to myself. And as they ran into the bottom bend, I sped up again. I didn't give them opportunity to react this time. I just flew around them and in front of the main stand I ran the most beautiful and probably even the fastest finish of my life. When I felt the finish tape on my chest, I was overjoyed'.

And so was Dana, with however a major caveat. The final of the women's javelin was due to begin concurrent with the 5000 metres, and as she records, the last thing she needed was the sort of cliff-hanger finale that Emil had stage-managed so adroitly. 'That´s terrible, she wrote in their autobiography, 'That Topek (his pet name) always makes it so exciting that the whole stadium is on its feet. When I see him chasing like that my knees are shaking. With that, I won't throw any distance at all'.

'I was trying to comfort her,' wrote Emil, 'telling her to stay calm, because she's lost before and I wasn't going to win the 5000 metres anyway. At the finish I recognized, to my delight, my mistake. When I looked around the stadium, I didn't see either Dana or the other javelin throwers. We met in the changing room after the award ceremony. I wanted to ask why the javelin had been delayed but I couldn't get a word in edgeways. She jumped all over me, she was so thrilled. "You really won it! That´s wonderful! Show me the medal!" And there she was, putting it into her bag. For good luck, she said. I wasn't even dressed after my shower when the coach ran in, yelling, "Dana threw 50 metres!" "She must have broken the national record with that," I said incredulously. "So she did," he said, "and even the Olympic one. Just imagine, right on the first throw! The others almost fainted when they saw it". And so

Dana won it with that first throw. It was really strange and I wasn't the only one who thought she threw it because she was excited by my victory. When I told her, she just smiled. "Oh yeah?" she said. "So go and excite some other girl if you're so smart. See if she'll throw a javelin 50 metres for you!'"

For Zátopek, the final leg of the hat-trick, or 'tiercé' as *L'Équipe* styled it – a common reference to the Tote, or Parimutuel bet on a treble (trifecta in the US/Australia) – was the marathon. Following the 5000 metres victory, Zátopek had gone to the training track to test out the sort of pace he needed to run in order to feature in the marathon. He couldn't believe it when the coaches kept telling him to slow down, that he was running far too quickly. So he decided the best option was to follow the favourite. The then world record holder was the UK's Jim Peters, who had finished eighth, over a lap behind Zátopek in the Olympic 10,000 metres at Wembley four years earlier. With his customary lack of inhibition, Zátopek sought out Peters on the start-line and introduced himself. His intention was to follow Peters, who had run his world record 2hr 20min 42sec in the celebrated 'Poly' Marathon in west London two months before. Peters' self-confessed tactic was to lead from the gun and kill off the opposition. Accordingly, the Englishman shot off and had a 100 metres lead on his pursuers, including Zátopek before the runners had even left the stadium. But, as with Peters' infamous collapse at the end of the Empire Games marathon two years later – having been eighteen minutes ahead at one stage – the increasingly warm conditions were going to put paid to his ambitions.

Zátopek had been leading the chase alongside the Swede Gustaf Jansson, and the pair caught the wilting Peters after 15 kilometres. Zátopek records that Peters had been amiable enough on the start-line, but when the neophyte asked the world record holder if he wasn't going too fast for the conditions, Peters, who clearly thought Zátopek was indulging in gamesmanship, replied, "Pace too slow," putting on a spurt as he said so, and crossing to the opposite side of the road to avoid any more impertinent questions. Shortly afterwards, Zátopek and Jansson began to pull away from Peters, who laboured on, finally dropping out before 35 kilometres.

After the problems of determining pacing, Zátopek's next question was about refreshment. When Jansson, who had been running marathons for at least two years, took a half-lemon at the 25k feed station, Zátopek pondered that one. 'They offered me some as well,' he wrote of the lemon. 'I didn't take it because I didn't have any experience of that. So only Jansson ate it. It doesn't matter, I said to myself, if he goes faster now, I'll eat three lemons at the next station. After about 500 metres there came a small hill. While I was running it quite easily, Jansson dropped back. I turned around and I saw that he was fading. That's the lemon, I thought. I won't eat anything! And so I didn't take anything right through to the finish'.

If you take a look at the marathon footage which, like the other races, is widely available online, you'll see that Zátopek, without a competitor to talk to starts chatting to the cameraman covering the race. He also rolls up his running vest, in an attempt to cool down. He smiled his way through the finish line in 2hr 23min 03sec, another Olympic record. A few seconds later, the Jamaican 4x400 metres relay team, which had just beaten the US quartet to gold in a world record time descended on Zátopek, hoisted him onto their shoulders, and carried him on a lap of honour round the stadium. The one thing that everybody noticed however was that running along the open road at what to him was little more than jogging pace, there was none of the head rolling, none of the arm wrestling, none of the Zátopek contortions. He exhibited perfectly relaxed, upright, fluid running style.

27.

I knew that Zátopek had been involved in a stand-off with the athletics authorities over the de-selection of a young colleague, prior to going to the Olympic Games in Helsinki in 1952. But I hadn't realised how serious it was. Helsinki was to prove Zátopek's greatest triumph, with a distance treble – golds in the 5000 metres, 10,000 metres, and marathon – that is unlikely ever to be repeated, for reasons I'll go into later. But, it seems that if he had not been successful in Helsinki, the likelihood is that he would have ended up in jail. It was my first interview with Dana, in summer 2014, which alerted me to the full extent of his selfless stand on behalf of Stanislav Jungwirth, and the potential repercussions that he might have suffered. It was the most animated that I saw Dana during our several hours of conversation. And she lapsed into English, the better to impress on me, "People don't realise how dangerous it was. They were executing people".

That sent me scurrying back to the search engines and the National Library history archive. But it turned out that there was an indication right outside the front door of the flat where I was staying. The principal thoroughfare at the end of the street, on which the Prague Marathon office is located, is named after Milada Horáková. A law graduate of the celebrated Charles University in Prague, Horáková joined the underground resistance as soon as the Nazis occupied Czechoslovakia. She was captured in 1940, and sentenced to death, commuted to imprisonment, firstly in the infamous Terezín (Theresienstadt) concentration camp, then in jails in Germany. After Liberation, she re-joined the Social Democrat party she had supported prior to the Occupation. She was elected to Parliament, but resigned her seat after the 'Victorious February' coup brought the Communists to power in early 1948.

Despite exhortations to leave the country, Horáková continued militating against the Communists, and was eventually arrested in late 1949. She was accused of leading a plot to overthrow the government and, with Soviet 'advisors' on hand stood trial with a dozen 'co-conspirators' in May 1950. A little over a week later, along with Jan Buchal, surrealist poet Záviš Kalandra and Dr. Oldřich Pecl, she was sentenced to death. Despite international appeals, including from such luminaries as Albert Einstein and Winston Churchill, she was executed, by strangulation, in Pankrác prison on June 27, 1950. She was 48 years old.

While this was probably the most extreme example of the murderous paranoia of the infant Czechoslovak Communist regime, for those who persist in the delusion that sport has no part of politics, consider the fate of the Czechoslovak ice hockey team. World Champions in 1947 (when future Wimbledon tennis champion Jaroslav Drobný scored nine goals), and again in 1949, they only lost the Olympic gold in 1948 on goal difference to Canada. The team was preparing to leave for London, to defend the world title in March 1950, when the trip was cancelled on the pretext that two journalists had been refused accreditation.

The players nonetheless turned up at the city centre pub, U Herclíků, to celebrate the birth of Jiří Macelis's son. According to one of the young stars, Gustav Bubník, they got angry at a Czech Radio report broadcast in the bar, giving a garbled story of their grounding. As the beer went down, the criticism of the regime mounted. The StB, the secret police turned up, and at least one of them got flattened for his pains. But the players, with one notable exception were all arrested, including Bohumil Modrý, who had not even been present that evening.

The players appeared in court shortly after the Horáková farrago, and were accused of being 'state traitors,' who were planning to defect - this despite the fact that they had had numerous chances to do so since the Communist take-over. Drobný had been the only one to do so, after a tennis tournament in Switzerland in 1949. Goaltender Modrý, considered the best in the world at that time, was sentenced to 15 years in prison. Bubník got 14 years, and ten other players received sentences between three months and 12 years. Most of them were sent to the notorious uranium mine at Jáchymov where, two decades later, Zátopek would work as a labourer. The majority of the hockey players received a presidential pardon five years later, although Modrý died within ten years, of prison-related complications. And it would take two decades before the national hockey team made any similar impact on the world scene.

Given a recent history such as this, if it was a gamble that he was taking prior to Helsinki 1952, Lieutenant Zátopek must have been confident that he held all the aces. He was already an Olympic champion - the first in Czechoslovak athletics history - having won the 10,000 metres, in London 1948. He broke his first world records, at 10,000 metres, in 1949. He went on to demolish the formerly unbeatable Finns, inheritors of the great Paavo Nurmi, on numerous occasions, including setting another 10,000 metres world record, in Finland in August 1950, three weeks prior to winning the European Championships 'double' - 5000/10,000 metres - by the proverbial street. The number of races he ran each season was, like his training, unconscionable. But he went into Helsinki, two days late, unbeaten in the Olympic distances for over three years. He was a folk hero, and an ostensible supporter of the regime, who could be used as a propaganda tool. Nevertheless, he had defied the authorities in the most blatant fashion.

He must have known that was treading a finer line than his increasingly outlandish training would ever suggest. Dana certainly knew. The Czechoslovak athletics federation, instructed by the regime, had determined that the young athletics hopeful, Stanislav Jungwirth would not travel to Helsinki. Jungwirth's father was an anti-Communist activist, who had been distributing tracts criticising the regime. Stanislav would pay the price for his father's indiscretions. Zátopek disagreed. Although a member of the military elite, he stood on principles which would re-emerge, equally publicly, throughout the events of the Prague Spring and the Soviet invasion 16 years later. He refused to go to Helsinki unless Jungwirth was restored to the team.

The management had assured Zátopek that Jungwirth would be on the same plane to Helsinki, but Zátopek wanted to check for himself. I've seen varying accounts of the stand-off, but at our first meeting Dana told me that when they boarded the dawn plane at Ruzyně, just outside Prague, Emil went looking for Stanislav. When he couldn't find the youngster, a heated argument ensued. Zátopek grabbed his bag, kissed Dana, did what he could to reassure her, and left the plane. He travelled back to the city, and went to find Jungwirth, who was languishing in his room in the athletes' quarters at the Strahov national stadium. "Come on," said Emil to the astonished youngster, "get your kit on, we're going running". And that's what they did, for the next two days; until the regime capitulated. Inevitably, the 'official' biography, *Zátopek, The Marathon Victor* (1954), by František Kožík, does not mention these extraordinary happenings. Kožík's only concession is the biblical understatement, 'Emil went to Helsinki in the second wave of the Czechoslovak team'. "I was in tears," Dana told me. "Emil was taking a big chance".

As we know, not only did Emil Zátopek run well at the Olympic Games in Helsinki 1952, he made history. On Day One, he successfully defended his 10,000 metres title, setting an Olympic record, and beating his 'shadow' Alain Mimoun of France by over 100 metres. Two days later, he qualified easily for the 5000 metres final, which he duly won another two days later, in another Olympic record. Barely an hour after that victory, Dana won gold in the javelin. Joking that the family tally of gold medals was 'too close' at 2-1, Zátopek ran the marathon, his first, on the final day of the Games. He won that too, again in an Olympic record.

Jungwirth, incidentally did not run well in Helsinki, going out in the semi-finals of both 800 and 1500 metres; and though he went on to break world records for the 1000 and 1500 metres, both in Zátopek's favourite stamping ground at Stará Boleslav, he was never really a championship runner, winning only one major medal, a bronze behind Roger Bannister in the European Championships 1500 metres in Berne 1954.

When Emil and Dana returned home from Helsinki, it wasn't to prison. It was to be whisked off on a tour, of schools, factories, offices, and other public places where the Olympic family heroes – they had won four of the seven Czechoslovak golds - could be fêted. Nevertheless, there was still a reckoning to be had. When all the initial fuss had died down, Lieutenant Zátopek was summoned to the Ministry of the Interior, for a meeting with the Army Chief of Staff, General Václav Kratochvíl.

Clearly not everyone in the Communist hierarchy was a goon. When he told me this story, Zátopek described Kratochvíl as, "a good man". I took this to mean that, like many people during those trying times, the General did the best he could in the circumstances. And, like Emil's exit from the plane, General Kratochvíl was clearly not averse to a bit of theatre himself. With Lieutenant Zátopek standing to attention on the other side of his desk, the General made much of studying a copy of *Rudé právo*, sporting the headline

Emil Zátopek's World Success, alongside which lay a document which Zátopek knew called for his censure for insubordination, ie the Jungwirth 'affair'.

The General couldn't understand it, he said, so he called in his secretary, and declared, "Look, I don't know much about sport. You'll have to fill me in: are there two Zátopeks?"

"No, Sir. There is only the one". "In that case then," replied General Kratochvíl with, as we can imagine, the ghost of a smile on his face, "this is nonsense". And he took up the proposal for exemplary punishment, and tore it in two. Zátopek was duly promoted to Major, and his enemies retreated.

28.

Some nicknames given to Zátopek

Cry-Baby Emil – by elder brothers, when confronted by dad's strap .

The Badger - when he had hair.

Emil the Second - before he started winning.

The Human or Czech Locomotive – stringing opponents out behind him like rail carriages.

The Bouncing Czech – due to his tortured running style.

The Galloping Major – when he was promoted in the army.

Satupekka – 'Fairytale Peter', Finnish play in his name after his Helsinki treble.

Jatopek – After winning the Sao Paulo San Silvestre (New Year's Eve) race in Brazil in 1952, locals began this play on his name – Jato, Portuguese for jet.

Saint Emil of Prague – emblematic of reverence for an athletic legend.

29.

When I met Zátopek in 1998, I had just finished the filming of a television documentary on the rise of Kenyan running. Since the Kenyans were enjoying widespread success using training regimes which owed much to Zátopek's solo initiative 50 years earlier, a documentary on the man who started it all was an obvious next project. I met Emil again the following year, by which time it was obvious that both his body and mind were failing. I lurched into action in early 2000, and began the project with a pre-Olympic visit to Australia, during which I interviewed the great Aussie distance runner, and Zátopek champion, Ron Clarke.

I'd first gone to Australia in 1985, ostensibly to attend the World Cup in Canberra, where the highlight was Marita Koch of East Germany running 48.60sec for 400 metres, a mark which still stands as a world record, and is likely to do so for years to come, thanks, like many other athletics world records to a variety of performance enhancing drugs. En route to Canberra, I stayed for several days in Sydney, and apart from stumbling on the Sleaze Ball, the annual gay festival, one of the best all-night parties I ever attended, I found Sydney as dull as a wet Sunday afternoon in an English provincial town in the 1950s. People were still smoking dope in restaurants, for God's sake. Fifteen years later, in the lead-up to the Olympic Games in 2000, I re-found Sydney, and it was as vibrant and culturally varied as any European or north American city with a cosmopolitan population.

Through the decade over the turn of the century, I was free-lancing for the *Financial Times* during a period when the newspaper was flirting with a sports section, and the travel page editor secured me a trip to Sydney, to survey the Olympic preparations. That allowed me to drive up to the Gold Coast, where Clarke had business interests, including the running of an exclusive resort, Couran Cove on South Stradbroke Island. He went on to become mayor of the Gold Coast for a dozen years.

I'd met Ron a couple of times when he was running upmarket sports clubs in the UK during the 1980s, and over ten years later he still looked in strapping health, despite having had heart valve surgery, a legacy, he maintained of running himself to a standstill in the 10,000 metres in the rarefied air of Mexico City at the Olympic Games in 1968. As multi-world record holder, he was favourite for Olympic gold in Mexico. He could only manage sixth, beaten by men he'd never heard of. One of the most distressing photos in athletics history is an image of him prostrate on the infield, being given oxygen by a medic who is in tears, believing him on the verge of death. It says much about the mind and mentality of the distance runner, that Clarke – like John Treacy of Ireland in Moscow 1980 and Steve Ovett in LA 1984 (after similar collapses) - went on to contest a follow-up Olympic event, in Clarke's case the 5000 metres, where he finished fifth.

We filmed a lengthy interview with Clarke, which began with him running up the gorgeous white sand beach of Couran Cove, with the Coral Sea white-caps breaking in the background. He could still run a few kilometres, he said, but the most galling thing for him was that he could barely keep with up with his elder brother Jack, a former 'Aussie Rules' footballer (like their father), rather than an ex-world record runner like himself. Despite his own pre-eminence as a distance runner - he had broken all the same records as Zátopek - Clarke was a one-man propaganda vehicle for Emil. He said it began back when he was a successful teenager, and world junior Mile record holder in the mid-fifties. Clarke became just as famous for lighting the Olympic flame at the Melbourne Games of 1956, when the magnesium from the torch sparked onto him, burning his arms and pock-marking his tee-shirt. Clarke made light of it, but as he said, he is probably still remembered more in Australia for that incident than for the 18 world records that he set in the 1960s.

Clarke's introduction to Zátopek came via a Melbourne neighbour, Les Perry, who was one of the world's leading distance runners at the time, and finished sixth, behind Zátopek's victory in the Olympic 5000 metres in the Helsinki 1952. "I didn't know Les at the time," said Clarke, "but he was the man who started all our (Australian) distance running, and he was an Emil Zátopek devotee. He absorbed the Zátopek personality and approach and hard work. And he was such an enthusiastic man, very much like Emil that way. He got Dave Stephens going, who broke the world Six Miles record. He got a whole club of athletes, Geoff Warren, Neil Robbins, all that Williamstown crowd, he was secretary of; he used to go out and mark the lines (on a grass track), and I mean, he was an international athlete, Australian champion. He'd mark the lines in the morning, and go out and run 'em in the afternoon, and take all the membership 'subs' at night time. Les was that sort of guy, in fact it was Les Perry, who got me back running again.

"When I started running as a junior, Les was one of those who encouraged me, and gave me the stories about Emil, and what a great personality he was, and how friendly he was, how many languages he spoke. He gave me all the info. When I then concentrated more on my family and academic career, and got going in business, I transferred to a house that was very close to Les. It was Les helped me move in, and he that came round to me and said, look, you should get back into running again. You're getting too old too young. I was only about 24 or so, and he said, come for a run, and I thought, here's this very old guy of 40, and looked about 60, and he grunted and groaned and wheezed as he was running up the hills around where we were living, and I couldn't keep up with him. And he had a mate who was just as old and just as decrepit, and I couldn't keep up with him either. And he was the local mayor.

"So in a way, it was Zátopek's personality that reflected through Les that got me going, that got Australian distance running going. And it was Les that got John Landy going more than anyone else. Les started getting Cerutty's camp famous (Percy Cerutty was the legendary coach of unbeaten miler Herb Elliott, Rome Olympic 1500 metres champion). Landy (Olympic 1500m, bronze medal, 1956) went to Cerutty's camp. He got Don McMillan going there, the whole regime that got Elliott going. The whole thing started with Les Perry meeting Emil Zátopek. Emil Zátopek really influenced them. He was the godfather of Australian distance running".

Despite lighting the Olympic cauldron, and being a minor personality himself at that time, Perry's stories had left Clarke so in awe of Zátopek and his achievements that when he encountered him in a Melbourne street one day during the '56 Games, he couldn't pluck up the courage to speak to him. "He got off a tram, and I wanted to go up to him and say hello to him, but he walked right past me". It would be almost a decade before Clarke encountered Zátopek again. And that meeting would eventually lead to one of the most endearing anecdotes in Olympic history.

30.

It takes many things to become a world class athlete, not the least of which is the will to succeed. Zátopek often said that his was, "an ordinary talent. I just worked hard". If it were only that simple! But what about being born at the right time? And I'm not simply referring to the collision of Zátopek's sporting maturity with a relatively fallow era in athletics achievement, following the depredations of World War II. I am talking, literally about his birth date.

One of the most intriguing interviews I ever did during my 30 years of athletics journalism was with Richard Hepworth, a schoolteacher from Bradford in Yorkshire, whose claim to fleeting fame came in the wake of one of his trainees' superlative performance at the celebrated Bislet Games in Oslo, in 1993. At 30 years of age, almost ancient for 800 metres men, the little known Martin Steele, also from Yorkshire won the Bislet 800 metres in 1min 43.84sec, a performance which ranked him second in the world that year, and still ranks fourth on the UK all-time lists, behind such luminaries as double Olympic champion and world record holder Seb Coe, world champion and record holder Steve Cram and Commonwealth champion Peter Elliott; and ahead of another 'great', Olympic champion and world record holder, Steve Ovett.

Steele had represented the UK several times before without distinction. But extraordinary though this performance may have been, the principal interest in his quantum leap came when it emerged that he had recently entrusted his coaching regime to Hepworth, who unashamedly revealed that he based his training theories on athletes' biorhythms. I took a three-hour drive north to Hepworth's home one late Sunday afternoon that summer, and spent a couple of hours alternately bemused and incredulous at what smacked of New-Age dilettantism. I wrote a tongue-in-cheek piece on Hepworth for the *Guardian* colour supplement, but was not entirely dismissive of his views, since there was much to support his ideas. Principal among these was that an athlete's birthdate had a crucial significance on his/her development. Hepworth maintained that in the northern hemisphere, autumn was the most beneficial period to be born for an athlete who would be competing in major competitions in summertime in the same hemisphere. A quick check of the names I've mentioned above – Coe, Cram, Elliott, Ovett - reveals that they were all born within a 16-day window, between September 29 and October 14. And another 'great' that I was close to, Saïd Aouita was born on November 2. As for Zátopek, he was born on September 19.

Another minor point of interest is that Zátopek was left-handed, that is until, as was common at the time, indeed until much later, he had it knocked out of him both at school and at home. He records it in his typically droll fashion in *As Told by Dana and Emil.* 'When I was still in blankets they made a little experiment with me. They put all kinds of things in front of me including different tools and money, so that I could show my preferences. I took a shoe hammer in my left hand immediately. Everyone was nodding, thinking I was going to be a shoemaker, but I was left-handed. This was underlined when I started eating by myself, throwing stones and hammering nails. Then I started getting called butterfingers, bumpkin, muff and I don't know what else. Fortunately I didn't understand those words back then.

'The biggest fuss with my being left-handed came at school. Learning to write, a classmate told the teacher I was using my left hand. Everyone came to look and at first I thought it was admiration, but then the teacher told the class I was the worst case he'd seen. He forced me to take a stone in my right hand and he started saying, 'Ah, ah, ah,' like you do at the doctor's, while twisting my ear at the same time. At home, dad stood above me with a ruler in his hands until I made a few illegible letters with my clumsy right hand. I felt it was unfair that I had to write with the same hand as everyone else. The worst was that, while I got A grades for everything else, I never got an A for writing.'

There is a long history of suspicion of left-handers. Folklore has it that Satan was cack-handed, and it was often a determinant in the fate of alleged witches. Even the Latin word for left, *sinister,* has come to mean, well... sinister. However, there is a disproportionate number of world class sportsmen and women who are caggie. It may be the sense of being different which propels many to do better. But in sports such as fencing (in particular), tennis and squash, it is logical, since the right hemisphere of the brain (which governs the left side of the body) reacts marginally faster than the left hemisphere. So one-on-one sports where the competitor or rival is very close, ie, fencing, squash, tennis, badminton, boxing, even baseball and cricket (bowler/pitcher to batsman/batter), players benefit from being lefties. The prime example is fencing where it seems that the advantage of being left-handed has been accepted for almost a century.

In the 1920s, Milanese fencing master and many times Italian champion, Giuseppe Mangiarotti converted his right-handed son to being a leftie, and Edoardo rewarded dad by winning six Olympic titles. Despite only an estimated 10 to 12% of the world's population being left-handed, in the elite of fencing and baseball that statistic rises towards 50%, and more; for example, 14 of the top 20 career batting averages in Major League Baseball history have been posted by left-handers. In tennis, table tennis and boxing, the percentage of left-handers is 20% or more. The French neuroscientist and academic, Guy Azémar is an advisor to l'INSEP, the national sports and physical education institute. He has spent years researching the subject. In a Q&A in 2013, with the online magazine *notrefamille.com*, destined to advise parents on what sport their children might practise, Azémar writes, 'The right hemisphere of the brain controls not only the left hand, but also our spacial awareness, whereas the left hemisphere controls language and writing.... (left-handers) benefit most in reaction times to the element of surprise between close protagonists with little distance between them - fencing, table tennis, boxing'.

'The lay-out of the brain is the same in right and left-handers, but some researchers have noticed that the link between the hemispheres is more developed in left-handers. Therefore there would be a greater transfer of information between the two hemispheres. There are examples of right-handed tennis players and fencers being forced to change the dominant hand due to injury. They frequently improve their performance'.

On the other hand (so to speak), Azémar says that there are certain disciplines, such as pole vaulting, discus and ice-dancing, where left-handedness is a distinct disadvantage. 'In sports which involve the coordination of the whole body.... very few left-handed people reach elite level. Right handers normally use their left foot as a 'marker'. That makes it difficult to effect reverse body rotation (for lefties)'. According to Azémar, 'in some countries, there is such fear of discouraging left-handedness that, without realising it, more left-handers have been created. It's certainly been the case in the USA where, over the last 30 years, we've seen a far higher percentage of left-handers than in Europe'.

However, according to the statistics, it seems that there are a significant number of left-handers in sports where there would be no advantage to be gained from right-hemisphere dominance. There is no evidence as far as I can see that runners benefit from being left-handed, apart from imparting a sense of 'difference'. With Zátopek in mind, I only have my own mini-survey to add. Paula Radcliffe, holder of the women's marathon world record, over seven minutes faster than Zátopek ever achieved, is left-handed. And in the decade during which Sebastian Coe, Steve Ovett and Steve Cram were the dominant milers, Olympic or world champions and world record holders, both Cram and Ovett were lefties.

31.

Stará Boleslav is a town some 30 kilometres from Prague; and a seminal location in the history of Central Bohemia and the Czech Republic. It was on the steps of the (now) Baroque church that Prince Václav (Wenceslas), Duke of Bohemia was murdered at the behest of his brother Boleslav in the tenth century. This is the same Wenceslas of Christmas Carol renown, though he was never a King, nor knowingly spotted a poor man gathering winter fuel. The martyred Václav became the patron saint of the Czech lands, and 400 years later Charles IV, the Holy Roman Emperor was a frequent visitor to Stará Boleslav. But the Hussite (religious) wars put an end to the status of the town, and the church was destroyed, only being rebuilt in the 17th century. Just after the turn of the current century, the St Wenceslas National Pilgrimage to the town was reinstituted, with a visit by Pope Benedict XVI, and is now the largest official celebration in the country of St Wenceslas Day, which doubles as Czech Statehood Day, September 28.

I was on a pilgrimage of a different sort. After a visit to the church, to view the Romanesque frescoes and Palladium (icon) of the Madonna, I walked the two kilometres through the fields to the tiny Houšťka stadium where Zátopek had broken several records, most famously the trio of 15 Miles, 25,000 and 30,000 metres, on the same afternoon, of October 26, 1952. It's an atmospheric location. The stadium is in the middle of a forest, and even Zátopek subscribed to the belief that the trees bordering the stadium provided more oxygen for the runner. He had broken the 10 Miles, 20,000 metres and one-hour records on the same track 13 months earlier; and would go on the following year, 1953, to set one of his 10,000 metres world records there.

Nowadays Houšťka boasts a splendid 400 metres tartan track, but back when Zátopek was in his pomp, it was just shy of 364 metres and, of course, cinders. Which means that all the distances had to be carefully re-calibrated; for example, Zátopek's 10,000 metres record was set not over the usual 25 laps of the track, but over 27½ laps.

In the 1940s and 50s, Houšt'ka was used as a training camp for various sports teams, and at that time, due to Communist connections with North Korea, the complex was named after Kim Il Sung. Nowadays there is sports resort nearby, and rooms for talented youngsters on the first floor of the stadium, above the changing rooms and bar/restaurant. It is an idyllic location, with a bust of Zátopek framed by bushes between the changing rooms and the track. There is only one small grandstand and the track is otherwise surrounded by barbeque areas among the trees. Right outside the stadium is a road circuit of around two and half kilometres, skirting a small wood, with several teenagers doing laps that late morning. This is where Zátopek brought Ron Clarke for a run through the forests when the Aussie visited in the mid-sixties.

After an hour soaking up the atmosphere, I set out to walk back to the twin-town of Brandýs nad Labem. By now, the sun was right overhead, and I was down to shirt-sleeves. There was no traffic, except for the occasional bicycle. With the unfenced fields and ripe yellow wheat in the foreground, and the spire of the Baroque church rising beyond, it felt like strolling through a nineteenth century Russian novel. When I got close to the adjacent town, I hit the river, and there was a guy in his sixties wading out of the water in his underpants. He nodded a silent, unembarrassed hello. A little further along the road, I caught the bus back to Prague.

32.

Some quotes attributed to Zátopek

"After all those dark days of the war, the bombing, the killing, the starvation, the revival of the Olympics was as if the sun had come out....I went into the Olympic Village and suddenly there were no more frontiers, no more barriers, just the people meeting together. It was wonderfully warm. Men and women who had just lost five years of life were back again." (Olympic Games, London 1948)

"Are we going too fast?" (To world record holder Jim Peters in the Olympic marathon 1952)

"I was unable to walk for a whole week after that, so much did the race take out of me. But it was the most pleasant exhaustion I have ever known"

"Men, today we die a little." (On start-line of the Olympic marathon 1956)

"If you want to run, run a hundred metres; if you want to experience another life, run a marathon"

"It's at the borders of pain and suffering that the men are separated from the boys."

"I was an ordinary runner, I just trained hard."

"I wasn't smart enough to run and smile at the same time".

"A runner must run with dreams in his heart, not money in his pocket."

"You can't climb up to the second floor without a ladder. When you set your aim too high and don't fulfil it, then your enthusiasm turns to bitterness. Try for a goal that's reasonable, and then gradually raise it."

"There is a great advantage in training under unfavourable conditions. It is better to train under bad conditions, for the difference is then a tremendous relief in a race."

"The athlete of today is not an athlete alone. He's the centre of a team - doctors, scientists, coaches, agents and so on."

"Great is the victory, but the friendship of all is greater."

33.

As part of my research, I read Michael Žantovský's thoroughly entertaining biography of fellow-dissident and intellectual, the playright-President Václav Havel. Like any good biographer, he paints Havel in all his colours, dark as well as light; and I particularly enjoyed his venomous asides about former Communist dignitaries, eg 'a nonentity named Novotný'. After the Velvet Revolution, Žantovský held several diplomatic posts, and when we met he was still Czech Ambassador to the Court of St James, ie the United Kingdom. Žantovský was equally forthright about Zátopek. "He had a big mouth, that occasionally got him into trouble, and then, sometimes, he used the big mouth to get himself out of trouble again".

Žantovský was not aware of the incident, but one such prime example came as a prelude to Zátopek's two world records in three days in mid-1954 when, in theory his career was on the cusp of decline. In spring that year, he had made history again, becoming the first Czechoslovak to win the celebrated *l'Humanité* cross country race in the Forest of Vincennes, on the eastern edge of Paris, an event sponsored by the French Communist daily newspaper; and as such, a rare opportunity outside of a major championship or the still popular two-nation matches to see eastern-bloc athletes competing in the west. Earlier in the season, Zátopek had encountered a young Ukrainian sailor from the Black Sea fleet, who was going to take over his 5000/10,000 metres crowns at the Olympic Games in Melbourne – one Vladimir Kuts. Volodymyr, in the Ukrainian version, was going to rule the distance running world from late 1954 through to 1957, but the youngster was still six months away from being a match for the master.

One of the biggest disappointments for athletes of my generation was that eastern-bloc athletes did not compete in the International Cross-Country, precursor to the World Cross. Because that would have altered the face of the competition, which was largely dominated from its inception in 1903 by the England team, with occasional victories, both individual and collectively, by the French and Belgians. The *Cross de l'Humanité* in 1954 was dominated by

Warsaw Pact countries – Zátopek won by a street, from the Pole Jerzy Chromik, with Kuts in third place. But it was a stroll down a different kind of street – la Rue Pigalle – that was going to get our man into a spot of bother.

'I got a great reception back at home for being the first Czechoslovak to win *l'Humanité*,' he wrote, 'Many of my friends wanted to hear all about Paris as well, and because I wanted to include everything I told them not only about the nice experiences but also some less noble ones, from my evening promenade on the famous Rue Pigalle. What I didn't know was that one of the people there was a journalist who published an account with some of his own embellishments. I found out about the article two months later in Brussels, when I was on my way to Paris again for another big international race. The Belgian police gave it to me to read in French together with a comment that for this criticism of Paris I wouldn't get a French visa. Once again, conclusive proof that he who has it in the legs doesn't necessarily have it in the head.' After hours of diplomatic to-ing and fro-ing, Zátopek's 'minder' was summoned to the French embassy in the middle of the night before the race, when he was finally able to pick up their visas. By dawn, reports Zátopek, they were walking down the rather less dangerous Rue Lafayette. The race was in Stade Colombes early evening that same day, and later, Zátopek reflected on what he referred to as the 'strange nature' of sporting performance.

'Sometimes, you prepare for a race as well as you can, and the result disappoints you. Other times you start a race feeling out-of-sorts, and you get a personal best. And that's what happened in Paris. Right from the start I ran away from the others and got such a lead that everyone got involved; the spectators were riveted, and all the other athletes ignored their events, and crowded to trackside. It was then that I started feeling that something special was on the cards. I increased my efforts and my last kilometre was the fastest. I ran through the line to huge applause, but that was nothing compared to what happened after the result was announced. My time of 13min 57.2sec had broken Gunder Hägg's twelve year old world record by one second'.

The Belgian athletics federation took advantage of his having to come back to Brussels to get the plane to Prague, to set up an impromptu 10,000 metres race two days later, thinking they might profit from his clearly superlative form. Despite a saturated track, the result of 24 hours rain beforehand, he did not disappoint. But, again he provided evidence of Žantovský's contention that he couldn't help having a big mouth. 'I was so certain of my good form that I said without due reflection that it would be a new record again.... I said a few words about it to Belgian radio and I invited everyone confidently to come and take a look at my next success. But it almost didn't happen'.

Nowadays, it is virtually impossible to witness a world record in a distance running event without the aid of pacemakers. Though there were pacers in Brussels on that wet evening on June 1, 1954, they only went as far as 3000 metres, and it is testimony to Zátopek's talent and tenacity that when they began sprinting their last lap, ie between six and a half and seven and a half laps (of the 25), he did not deter or follow them, but persevered, not without difficulty, and ran out with the first sub-29 minute 10,000 metres in history – 28min 54.2sec. 'The next day I had a fever as bad as if I was sick,' he wrote, 'but it was worth it for the performance. But I would never brag about my good form before a race again. Never again'.

But, according to their autobiography, the best was yet to come. Dana had frequently reminded him that the ultimate imprimatur of his distance running superiority would be to add the one thing that was missing from his CV - breaking Hägg's 5000 metres world record, to add to his four Olympic golds and now five 10,000 metres world records. She even taunted him by saying she would bow down in front of him publicly if he achieved it. The reckoning was nigh. But when she was one of the group that greeted him at the airport back in Prague, she asked timidly if she might not kow-tow back at home. He insisted that she do it publicly, "as you promised". 'And so Dana really bowed down in front of me, all the way down to the ground. And because there were so many photographers around, it was in all the newspapers the following day. And I have saved the pictures, just in case anyone ever tells me that I never achieved anything through running'.

34.

I'd been told by historian Pavel Kosatík that there was one man who had dared to match Zátopek in his 100 x 400 metres madness. But Ivan Ullsperger said though they had done a lot of 400 metres reps, he didn't think they'd done that many, though they had run 53 kilometres on that particular day. Now that is more than 10 kilometres, or six and a half miles further than a marathon, most of it at an elevated pace; which is to say that this was compounding a felony - small wonder that Ullsperger collapsed at the end of the session, and couldn't get out of bed the following day.

Ullsperger was the third training contemporary of Zátopek I interviewed. A slight, sprightly man, despite walking with the aid of crutches, we met at the magnificent sports centre beside the local football ground in his home town of Jablonec nad Nisou in north Bohemia, close to the three-way border with Germany and Poland. At 84, he was half a dozen years younger than Roudný and Kořán, and like the latter he had begun his teenage sports career as a cyclist, but switched for a far more prosaic reason than the assassination of a Hitler favourite by hit-men on bicycles. "Originally, I never wanted to be a runner, I preferred cycling. I used to cycle to school, and it was a long way, but one day I had my bike stolen. So I decided to run, that way there was nothing to steal. I was 17 years old.

"My original idea was to be a marathon runner. I knew how fast Zátopek was running 10k, in thirty minutes. So I tried to run a kilometre in three minutes, and keep up that pace as long as possible. But it took me until 1952, before I could run three kilometres in under nine minutes. I was still living in Jablonec, but later that year, I went to Prague to begin my military service. I didn't expect to meet Zátopek, though I knew he was an army man. When I went for my medical at the army hospital, the doctor actually told me, you have a strong heart. You should be able to run like Zátopek. I began training with a coach who trained Jungwirth, but eventually, in autumn '53, I joined Emil's training group. He would give different training to different people in his group, five times 200 metres to some, ten times 400 metres to others. But he said to me, Ivan, you are young, so you can do all of this training".

So quickly did Ullsperger develop that he ran for Czechoslovakia in East Germany the following year, and was also selected for the European Championships in Berne. But, given that he had been raised in Austria during the War, and still had family in Germany, initially he wasn't permitted to race in the west, another example of the official paranoia which prevailed through the mid-fifties. But he was finally given permission to join Zátopek in the *Cross de l'Humanité* in Paris 1955, presumably because the event was a promotion of the Communist party daily. It was a soggy baptism. Torrential rains had reduced the course to thick mud. But Ullsperger acquitted himself splendidly, as Zátopek himself records in his co-autobiography with Dana.

'The lightweights only sunk in up to their ankles. On the other hand Kuts, who had put on more than ten kilos during the winter on his already oversized body, couldn't get along with the terrain at all. If I'd had time for it during the race, I would have felt sorry for him. He was beaten by quite ordinary runners, and ended up 13th. The featherweight (Jerzy) Chromik was like mercury. He danced away from us by a distance on the penultimate lap. But it was a mistake, he told me after the race; he thought he was on the last lap. When he heard he'd got another two kilometre lap to do, he was deflated. I told Ivan Ullsperger who was running alongside me to chase him down. I didn't think I could do it myself. Because Ivan was our youngest runner and had great respect for me, he did as I asked and went after him. It looked so easy that I sped up myself, and we caught Chromik almost at the same time. When Chromik saw us, he woke up, and sped off again. But this time, I was ready for him. I saw he was tired and I paid him back for each of his bursts with some accelerations of my own, exhausting him even more. We were running faster and faster and the spectators were going crazy. Even though he was tired, for a while I wasn't sure I could beat him. We were running neck and neck. With 400 metres to go, it was still not decided. But fifty metres from the line he cracked'. Zátopek won from the Pole with Ullsperger third.

Despite that success, Ullsperger maintained that training with Zátopek was harder. "We would do sessions with Emil, but we could never keep up with him. It was OK at the start of each 400 metres, but after halfway, Emil would go away from us. I managed to stay with him occasionally. Once, when I was following him, he got faster and faster; and afterwards, he said, Ivan, we ran a little too fast that time. Emil was a sort of older brother to me. I had an older brother of my own, but we were separated because of the war. Emil was a very pleasant, sensible person. One day he asked me what time it was, and I said I don't know, I don't have a watch. I'm saving up to buy one. The day afterwards, Emil came and gave me a watch that he'd got from the Helsinki Olympics.... When I left the army, I didn't have anywhere to stay. I was sleeping in little hotels. Emil insisted that I come and live with him and Dana. He asked her first, of course. That was one of the best times of my life. But after a while, my mother and others said it's not right to live with a married couple like that, you're in the way. I could see she was right, so I told Emil. He was sad, but he agreed it was probably best. So I left and came back home.

"He was a fantastic guy, it didn't surprise me that he supported Dubček, and signed the *2000 Words Manifesto*. I wouldn't have done it, but he did. I would have told him not to sign, that it would change nothing, but I didn't see him at that time. He was a very gentle guy, who loved talking with people; sometimes he talked too much".

Ullsperger beat Zátopek twice in 5000 metres races in 1955, when Emil had a dip in form, but he had another, more exciting victory, by one second in the national championships 10,000 metres in 1957. But the younger man didn't have much luck with international championships. Prevented by paranoid officials from running in the European Championships in 1954, he was selected for the Olympic Games in Melbourne 1956, but got a severe adverse reaction to tetanus injections and couldn't go. But his career lasted far longer than any of his contemporaries. He did eventually graduate to the marathon and other long distances, and continued running in masters' or veterans' competitions, competing in the UK and winning a 25k world masters title for his age group in Tokyo in 1975.

I'm not sure if it was due to his deafness or simply an insistence on telling it his own way, but in close to two hours, admittedly through an interpreter, Ullsperger never answered a question directly. But it was thoroughly entertaining. Despite his years, he was a vivacious interviewee, and when we finished, he bounced out of the office we had been using and sped across the concourse of the sports centre. We had to run to catch him up, and present the crutches that he'd left propped behind the office door. He peered at them, as if he never seen them before, smiled and shrugged, put them under his arm, said goodbye once more, and sped off again.

35.

The unexpected world records at the end of the 1954 season induced a bout of reflection on the nature of his disciplines for Zátopek. 'It's nice to be a world record holder. You have to work really hard to better everyone else, but after that you're a hero even if you simply rest on the laurels. When I was experiencing happy moments like that after my feat in Paris, I had the feeling that we distance runners are appreciated more than most. There are such big differences in the athletics disciplines. Just imagine the high jump! The spectators barely have time to cheer if the bar stays on. Only after that they can talk to each other about what it was they saw in the flash of a second.

'The 5000 metres, on the other hand is completely different. Each lap passes relatively slowly, people have something to watch and think about it, reflect on as it happens; they can even quietly advise the runners; they know the best is yet to come. And if it's a really thrilling race whose drama can be enhanced by the stadium announcer, the spectators see an enthralling competition they won't forget. I'm not surprised that it inspires them, and makes them think that something as simple as running around a big grass field over and over again is 'incredible'. If you break a record in a completely unknown and distant country, they will still carry you out on their shoulders; and they'll write you indelibly into sports history. It's worth the training and you can see why so many people make the effort to excel.

'And they're succeeding more than they did 20 or 30 years ago. More knowledge, better scientific training methods, more contacts and exchange of experiences, this all accelerates the evolution of the sports performances. While Paavo Nurmi used to run records all over the world without competition, today the situation is opposite. There are several athletes competing for domination in just one discipline. Many times they're close to a record but they seem to lack the nerve to reach out for it; as if it were out of respect for the performance they long thought unattainable. But if someone does it, and shows them the way, that gives them the courage to do it themselves – and the floodgates open.

'Sometimes you can predict such changes. Storm clouds start to form over certain disciplines. That's what it looked like in 1954 for Hägg's record. Anufriev, Kuts, Pirie and Kovács all ran faster than me at 5000 metres the previous year. I knew that if I didn't break the record before one of them, it would be lost to the younger generation. That's why I was so pleased with my record in Paris. I took my only chance to become king of all of the distances from five to 30,000 metres. I felt like I was coming to the end of my road. Now you can fight among yourselves, I thought when I saw the other 5000 metres runners. I've confirmed my place in history, now I can calmly run my 10,000 metres races; there are not so many great athletes there. I can go undefeated for a few years more, or so I thought.'

Though Zátopek's competitive decline may be traced from 1954, it was as much the rise of those younger abler contenders as a demonstration of his failing powers, because he was still winning more than he was losing, often with superlative times. The emergence of Soviet distance runners like Kuts and Anufriev were inevitable from such a huge country whose government clearly recognised the propaganda value of elite sports performance. Chataway and Gordon Pirie came from a great British middle and long distance running tradition. But Hungary was another matter. It was the sporting heyday for the (comparatively) tiny central European country, which dominated football through the early fifties, until the unaccountable defeat, after leading 2-0 at half-time, by West Germany in the World Cup final in Berne 1954. But there were also a half dozen world class Hungarian runners – led by Sándor Iharos, József Kovács, László Tábori and István Rószavolgyi – some setting world records post-Helsinki. All of that would be de-railed by the Soviet invasion in late 1956 (though the Hungarian water-polo squad would have their say at the Melbourne Olympics a month later, literally battering the Soviet team to defeat, 4-0).

Having presumed he could go undefeated for years at 10,000 metres, Zátopek lost his very next race at the distance, thus conceding his long unbeaten run (since 1948) by a whisker to Kovács in Budapest early in 1954. Three months later, however, he easily outwitted Kovács in the European Championships, also in Berne, even running under 29 minutes again, in defending his title. But, as he had suggested, the 5000 metres proved a race too far. Kuts ran away with the title, breaking Zátopek's three months old world record into the bargain, with 13min 56.4sec. To rub it in further, Chataway nipped Zátopek at the line.

Chataway did the same to Kuts in London a few weeks later – breaking the Ukrainian's world record - in a race that has stayed in the folk-memory of many Brits of a certain age, since it was the first live television athletics transmission, and it helped win Chataway the first *BBC Sports Personality of the Year* award, even beating his pal, Sir Roger Bannister's epoch-making feat of running the first sub-four minute Mile earlier in the year. For the record, Bannister won the European 1500 metres in Berne, while Dana won the first of two successive European golds. Kuts went straight from London to Prague, no less, and retrieved his 5000 metres world record within days. Giving full credit to Kuts, Zátopek records, 'During our race I felt more like a spectator than a rival. After the first lap he was 40 metres ahead of me; and by the last lap at least four times more. He broke the world record with 13.51.4. I was able to win the 10,000 metres the next day against Anufriev, but that couldn't compare with Kuts' performance.'

Though admittedly in decline, he was still running an inordinate number of races. In 1955, he contested a dozen 5000 metres, and a half dozen 10,000s, winning more than half of them. But he wanted to finish the season with a flourish, which he duly did by retrieving the little run 25,000 metres track record from the Estonian marathon runner, Albert Ivanov. It was his final world record. And in what was to become a feature of their lives for the next half a dozen years, Dana and Emil took off for a trip to India at the end of the year. According to journalist Štěpán Škorpil, the sports authorities did a deal with the Zátopeks where the couple received a percentage (doubtless small) of the fees from foreign countries/organisations, for their personal appearances and coaching expertise.

In their autobiography, Dana makes much of an encounter Emil has with an Indian fortune-teller, who gets angry with him because he's bought the cheapest prediction from the seer's table. And when he refuses to add to the one rupee he's paid for banalities, the fortune-teller puts a curse on him; or as Dana puts it, using his pet name, "Topek bought the cheapest one because he is stingy.... The angry fortune-teller was screaming another prophecy at him for free, 'You're too comfortable and lazy for your own good! You're never going to do anything with your life". Most of their appearances involved demonstrations and coaching by Dana, and often a solo run by Emil, since the locals were too overawed to compete against him. But when they got to Patiale in Punjab after Christmas, there were some takers for 5000 metres against the former world record holder. Maybe they were told he'd be running immediately after a huge lunch, which turned out to be the case, and it afforded Dana more fun at Emil's expense. This time, he tells the tale.

'So we both enjoyed the good food and went straight to the stadium from the banquet. Once the Maharaja was seated on the tribune with his company, they called me to the start. I didn't want to run at all, so I thought I'd begin quickly to put the others off, and that would be that. So I did, and by the second lap there was no one behind me. It was clear I didn't have to try very hard. So I was running effortlessly towards a distant victory. Even the spectators thought so too, since they stopped clapping after a few laps. That's good, I thought, I can win easily, even on a full stomach. I was into the last kilometre when suddenly the clapping started up again. At first I thought it for someone famous arriving in the stadium, then I saw two shadows on the track in front of me. I turned around and there he was – the best Indian.

'I started cursing myself for running so casually that he caught me. If he speeds up, he could beat me, I thought. The applause grew louder, and I turned around to see that there were now three of them right behind me. You can bet I wasn't going to wait for the finishing straight now. I sped up just like at the Olympics when I ran the last lap flat out. But they did the same. I was sprinting as fast as I could, with the spectators yelling now. But I couldn't drop them. At the finish line the best of them was almost level with me, and I only won by a hairsbreadth. "How stupid," I said to Dana, "to relax, and run so slowly that they caught me. I almost lost by trying to be too smart". "How come," replied Dana, with surprise. "You didn't know? After two laps, they went and sat on the grass, and only joined in again with two laps to go!" '

36.

Throughout the century of amateur athletics, the stringent rules governing the sport resulted in many people getting banned for what was usually claimed as, 'excessive expenses'. The most famous examples were the great Nurmi, who was thus prevented from a potential climactic farewell in the marathon at the Los Angeles Olympics in 1932, and the celebrated Swedes Gunder Hägg and Arne Andersson in the middle of the next decade. In neutral Sweden during the War, Hägg and Andersson's rivalry had brought the Mile world record within a whisper of four minutes, and had they not been banned in 1946, they would very likely have gone under four minutes eight years before Roger Bannister did the trick.

The post-War political alignments threw up another element in the debate. The Soviet-bloc claimed that the US college system, with its low academic standards was simply an excuse for full-time time training of athletes. The USA and the west in general responded by claiming that military service in the eastern bloc did the same thing. Both sides were essentially claiming that the other was professional. They both had a point. We've already seen how when civilian runners dared to beat Zátopek at home, his commanding officers demanded that he train full-time in order to avoid any further embarrassment to the Armed Forces. When Zátopek broke Hägg's 5000 metres world record in 1954, an editorial in the Swedish daily *Aftonbladet* asked why similar status could not have been afforded their own heroes a decade earlier. The sports editor, masquerading under the pen name of GIN wrote, 'Hägg was but 27 years old when he was declared a professional. This means that he should have had his best years as a runner still ahead of him. No doubt Zátopek, who was made a Major on account of his athletic achievements, has had much larger economic gains than Gunder could ever dream of. What really was there to stop us from having a Major Hägg touring the country and propagandising? In that case, he would probably be holder of several Olympic gold medals by now...'

As for 'economic gains,' larger or smaller, I would simply point out that when I interviewed Hägg and Andersson over a decade ago, they made it clear that they earned (under the table) huge sums of money for their exploits, sometimes 5000 kroner per race, the equivalent of the average annual national wage in Sweden at the time. And like Nurmi earlier, Hägg had also run on the profitable US indoor circuit, in his case braving the German U-boats in the Atlantic to get there. For a broader debate on the subject, consult the chapter in my book, *The Perfect Distance: Ovett & Coe, The Record Breaking Rivalry*. I am no apologist for amateurism or indeed Communism, but Gaston Meyer, the celebrated editor of *l'Équipe* at that time has an endearing anecdote about Zátopek's 'financial exigencies'. The story appears in Pierre Naudin's *Le Terrassier de Prague*. 'It was a while ago, probably 1947. Zátopek had been invited to run in the annual cross country, organised by *l'Echo d'Alger*, whose Paris correspondent was the former high-jump champion, Pierre Lewden. He'd invited me to join them for dinner at Hotel du Printemps, near Gare St Lazare, during the stop-off in Paris. I was introduced to a cheerful, charming young man who had a working knowledge of our language. Pierre Lewden, knowing the trade secrets of athletics wanted to know what his 'exigencies' were. Zátopek's reply was so astonishing that I have never forgotten it. "I run for my own pleasure, and nothing more, but if you insist, bring me two kilos of oranges. We don't have any in Prague".'

I don't doubt that later in his career, when he was going to races like the San Silvestre in Sao Paulo and the Lasarte cross country in San Sebastian that there was appearance money and other financial incentives, but since he was almost always accompanied by a minder, it may be that his share was little more than pocket money. TV journalist Škorpil recalls Emil saying to him once, entirely without rancour, 'You know, Štěpá, if I had one crown for every autograph I've signed, I'd be a millionaire". When he told me this, Škorpil added, "and if it was nowadays, he'd be a multi-millionnaire". And he quoted the rumour that Usain Bolt had received half a million dollars for appearing in the Golden Spike meeting in Ostrava in 2014. Emil and Dana were two of the first athletes ever to be sponsored by *Adidas*. Nowadays, that would also involve substantial sums of money, with bonuses for medals and other successes. But, as Dana told me in 2016, "Adidas was very good to us, but back then there was no money. It was only shoes, then later clothing, when they started making that".

37.

One of the popular tales about Zátopek, up there with running in boots and holding his breath 'til he passed out, is that he would train carrying Dana on his back. He did run in boots in the early days, but only in the snow when canvas shoes would have been useless, but like holding his breath, the stunt with Dana was a one-off, simply for a photograph according to her; and it proved costly. It provoked a hernia, which necessitated an operation, just six weeks before the Olympic Games in Melbourne. He didn't even bother to defend his 10,000 metres title, realising that his time on the track was past, at least in major championships. Even in the marathon, he must have doubted his chances, because when he learned that Mimoun was planning to emulate him, and try to win the Olympic marathon in his first attempt at the distance, he told Mimoun, "this time Alain, it's you". He was right. It was time for his 'shadow' to emerge into the sunlight.

As mentioned earlier, Mimoun was as much of a 'character' as Zátopek. A dynamic, ebullient man who, like Zátopek could have represented his country, adoptive in his case, in talking contests as well as running ones. Had it not been for Zátopek, Mimoun would be remembered as one of the greatest athletes in Olympic history. He finished second to Zátopek in five major championship races; the Olympic 10,000 metres in 1948, the European 5000 and 10,000 metres in Brussels 1950, and the same distances at the Olympic Games in Helsinki 1952. Yet he seemed to bear no malice, indeed quite the reverse. The one race where he thought he had the measure of Zátopek was in the 5000 metres in Helsinki. "I thought I had him; we dropped him with 300 metres to go, and I felt I was going to pass (Herbert) Schade and (Chris) Chataway. I was waiting for the finishing straight, and that was my mistake. Zátopek guessed correctly what I was going to do, and he passed on the bend, Bang! He was away, one tenth, two tenths, that was enough, and he won again. I was right behind, but second again. He was happy to be Olympic champion again, but I was equally happy, as if I'd won it. There's a great photo of us on the infield, embracing like lovers. There was nobody like him".

Mimoun was injured for the Euro Champs of 1954, in Berne, Switzerland, where Zátopek again won the 10,000 metres, but finished third to Vladimir Kuts and Chataway in the 5000 metres. But Mimoun would have his day, finally, in 1956 at the Olympic Marathon in Melbourne. He was 36 years old. Having won Olympic silver twice in succession behind Zátopek in the 10,000 metres, he used the race as a warm-up this time, finishing twelfth. "Everybody said I was too old, nobody thought I would win, not even *L'Équipe*. They gave me three lines. But Zátopek knew. I said, Emil, you're the strongest, but that saintly man, I always call him that, that saintly man, he said, no, this time, Alain, it's you. Now I don't like it when someone says that, I'm superstitious. But he repeated, Alain, it's you".

And so it proved. This time Zátopek was no match for Mimoun and another old friend, the Yugoslav Franjo Mihalić. In torrid heat, approaching 40C out on the open road, according to Mimoun, he ran away from the field and won in 2hr 25min. "I was still worried about Emil passing me, even though I knew he wasn't on form. When I finished, I stayed standing. I wanted to lie down, but I stayed upright, waiting. I thought, maybe he's second, but it was Mihalić. I was happy for him. He fell to the ground, and I thought, perhaps third? No, it's Karvonnen (Veiko, of Finland). Fourth? No, a Korean (Lee Chang-hoon). Jesus! Fifth, a Japanese (Yoshiaki Kawashima). He came in sixth. A great champion. The crowd applauded him like they'd applauded me. That's sport for you, as if he'd won. He saluted the crowd, but he didn't know that I'd won. It was the first time I'd ever beaten him. He fell to his knees, and I went over and said, 'Emil, listen, you were right, I'm Olympic champion. I won'. And I looked at this saint – I always call him a saint – it was like he was waking from a dream. 'Really?' he says, and he gets up, stands to attention like the soldier he was, takes off his cap, and salutes me. 'I'm happy for you,' he says, and then he kissed me. To me, that was worth all the money in the world".

38.

One of the most endearing Cold War sports stories was the love affair, and subsequent marriage of the Zátopeks' Olympic colleague, discus thrower Olga Fikotová to the US hammer thrower Harold Connolly*. The pair had met just prior to the 1956 Olympic Games in Melbourne, where they both won gold medals; and their obvious attraction to each other made headlines. But given this happened shortly after the Soviet invasion of Hungary, Cold War paranoia, still rampant in Czechoslovakia was not going to make their union easy. They barely had a common language, she spoke schoolgirl English, and Connolly had a smattering of German, from his competitions there in the past. After another trip to Germany the following year, Connolly turned up in Prague, where the couple planned to get married. However, they needed a permit for marriage to a foreigner. When sports officials tried to put Fikotová off, saying she was a traitor, she enlisted Emil's help to talk to then President, Antonin Zápotocký. In an interview with Czech radio, on a visit to Prague, in 2008, Fikotová recalled, "The next day, I received a note from his office, saying that he'd granted me an audience…. He said, 'I really can't help you very much, because different offices make the decisions…. but all I can do for you is to put in a kind word"… a few days later we received a permit'.

In a preview of Věra Čáslavská's 'celebrity' marriage to Josef Odložil immediately after the Mexico Olympics 11 years later, an estimated crowd of 30,000 people turned up to the Old Town Square in Prague to see the wedding, some of them, said Fikotová, "because they'd never seen Dana and Emil Zátopek, who were our witnesses; and some came to see the American who'd come to Prague". But the hardliners got their revenge on Fikotová. When she applied to return to Prague in order to qualify for the European Championships in 1958, she was told she was no longer a citizen, and apparently newspapers carried stories that she had refused to represent Czechoslovakia. She applied for US citizenship, and represented Uncle Sam at four more Olympic Games, even carrying the flag at the Opening Ceremony in Munich 1972. "In Mexico City (1968 Olympics), she recalled, "It was interesting when I met a group of

Czech athletes... They all knew me, or had heard of me, and they started talking to me. One said to me, 'Alright, how was it, did you really fly the coop, or did they give us a pack of lies about you?' I told them that I hadn't run away, and told them what had happened. It was only then that people began to understand that, in fact, I wasn't allowed to compete".

* Since no book on athletics is complete nowadays without reference to performance enhancing drugs, I should mention that Hal Connolly was the first athlete to testify to a US Senate Committee (in 1973) that he took steroids back in the day. Such drugs were not banned in international athletics or the Olympic Games until the mid-1970s.

39.

In all my years in athletics, now more than fifty, I don't think I've ever heard the expression, 'Philosophy of Running'. But that effectively is what Ron Clarke outlined when I sat down for a lengthy chat with him at the Couran Cove Resort he was managing in early 2000. The inspiration, indeed, foundation of that philosophy was, as you will know by now, Emil Zátopek. As I mentioned earlier, Clarke had been inducted into the Zátopek 'mystique' while still a junior in Australia, by an older runner, Les Perry, who had finished sixth behind Zátopek in the epic Olympic 5000 metres final in Helsinki 1952. It wasn't so much Zátopek the champion that enchanted Clarke it was Zátopek the personality, his attitude to life and to his running, which were indivisible. "He believed most importantly in competition," said Clarke, of his hero. "To me, the thrill of competition is when you meet somebody at their best, at their best distance, in their country, and you have a go at beating them. Now, if you're a 10,000 metre specialist, and they're a 5000 metre specialist, you get more thrill running against them in a 5000 metres, and taking the risk, not knowing who's going to win than racing him in a 10,000, when you know the odds are on your side. And that's how I raced.

"Zátopek raced people for the race's sake, for the competition's sake. He'd lead in order to get the race moving. He'd give advice to (Herbert) Schade in German, he'd take the pace for him. He wasn't not trying to win, but he was trying to win against the best, when they were at their best, and he never made excuses if he got beaten. He'd never say, oh, someone was sitting on me, or I had a bad cold, or whatever. He raced, and anybody up there is fair game, and that's why I believe competition is all about not protecting unbeaten records, or hating your opponent, or sheltering, and saying it must be like this, or it being the most important thing in the world, or whatever. "The race is over, then it's over, and you're looking forward to the next one and another one. And Zátopek preached this, and it's what I've tried to preach, and Les Perry preached it to Australia. The only fly in the ointment in Australia was Percy Cerutty, who was against everything. I'm so anti that. Too much emphasis is placed on Olympic golds. Sure Olympic gold's important, sure I'd like to have won one, and anybody'd like to have won one. But it's only a race. There's a whole career out there, there's a lot of time. There's 12 years of Kenyans that never got to the Olympics. One mistake and you don't get to compete in the Olympics. You mean to say you don't have a whole career, because you got an injury before the Olympic Games that your whole career's wiped out for some reason".

The Kenyan reference is to successive Olympic boycotts in 1976 and 1980 which deprived, among others, the quadruple world record holder Henry Rono from Olympic competition. However, my initial reaction when I heard Clarke's apologia was that, for all its admiration, indeed adulation of Zátopek, it was still the post-career rationalisation of someone who never won a gold medal. But I was ignoring the wider context. And the clue is in Clarke's criticism of Percy Cerutty, a man who had a huge impact, firstly on Australian athletics in post-war years, and then after he coached Herb Elliott to Olympic 1500 metres gold (in a world record) in Rome 1960, on the rest of the athletics world. My contemporaries and I treated his most successful book, *Athletics, How to Become a Champion*, published in the wake of Elliott's successes as if it were holy writ. Re-reading in later years, I recognised it has passages that wouldn't be out of place in *Mein Kampf.*

I never met Cerutty, so I can't give you a first-hand account, but these extracts from the *Australian Dictionary of Biography*, written by Cerutty biographer and journalist Harry Gordon will give you a flavour of the man...

Prickly and argumentative, Cerutty sometimes attempted to taunt the best out of his athletes. He said that he needed to enter their personalities. Some, like Landy, resented the intrusion and left; Cerutty never forgave them. Although Landy achieved his greatest success after breaking away, he always acknowledged a debt to Cerutty's early inspiration and conditioning. Elliott, his greatest pupil, absorbed all the Cerutty teachings. As Herb matured, he was able to laugh at his mentor's excesses, but he also wrote: 'Percy helped me . . . by releasing in my mind and soul a power that I only vaguely thought existed'.

Cerutty saw himself as a visionary with a noble mission. Some observers accepted his own view that he was a genius of sorts; others branded him an

exhibitionist, a crackpot, a nuisance and a publicity-seeker. His behaviour was
often unconventional: he stood on his head at a garden party, danced a jig on
championship arenas, challenged the chairman of a television panel to a fight,
was evicted often from Commonwealth and Olympic Games villages, and
wound up in police custody as Elliott scored the triumph of his career by
winning the gold medal in the 1500 metres at the 1960 Olympics in Rome.

As you can tell, 'Perce' as he was known in Aussie-speak was what some
would call a 'character', others a 'pain in the arse'. All the same, I wish I had
met him. Emil and Dana did meet Cerutty on at least two occasions, and in
their co-autobiography, Emil is very funny about 'Perce' in his downbeat
elliptical fashion. Their first meeting was in Helsinki 1952, and Emil records,
'In the evening the excitable coach from Australia, Percy Cerutty, came to see
me. They called him 'Coach' because he had it written on his tracksuit'. Emil
omits the fact that Cerutty outstayed his welcome and Emil, generous as ever,
offered him his own bed and retreated to sleep outside on a balmy night. But
a Czech official found Cerutty and kicked him out. Emil was a little more
deprecating in describing an afternoon spent with Cerutty following the
Melbourne Olympics four years later. 'Coach Cerutty took us around a
beautiful botanic garden, walking so quickly that we were barely able to keep
up with him. He was even jumping on the grass, on precious bushes and
flowerbeds of exotic flowers that we'd never seen in our lives. We asked him
whether that was allowed. Excitedly, 'Coach' explained eagerly that, on the
contrary it was strongly recommended for his athletes. I couldn't explain this
attitude any other way than that the Australians just don't have as much respect
for precious flowers as we do'.

It's clear that Cerutty's re-invention of himself after a nervous breakdown
had instilled an overdose of super-ego, or the Nietzschean concept of the
superman. And this is what irked Clarke and the likes of John Landy, who had
left Cerutty's training camp after one piece of public criticism, while never
failing to credit 'Perce' for helping his development. But if anyone personified
the alter-ego, as it were, to Cerutty, it was Landy. And Clarke has special reason
to admire Landy, as do many Australians of a certain age. Landy had competed
without distinction in the Olympics Games in Helsinki 1952. And it was partly
Cerutty's criticism of what he saw as Landy's lack of competitive spirit in

Finland that caused the future world record holder to withdraw from Cerutty. But Landy was another who had fallen under Zátopek's spell in Helsinki, and he wanted to trial the Czech's practice of interval training, which was at variance with Cerutty's methods. It evidently suited him, since two years later and within six weeks of Roger Bannister running the first sub-four minute Mile (3min 59.4sec), Landy ran 3min 57.9sec, a record which lasted over three years.

Another two years later, in the Olympic Trials of 1956 – with the Games coming up in their home town of Melbourne - Ron Clarke clipped someone's heels mid-race in the Mile, and fell. Running immediately behind him at that point, Landy trod on Clarke's arm as he tried to vault the youngster. Landy stopped and went back to help Clarke to his feet, making sure he was OK, before taking off again. Reports at the time suggest that Landy lost between five and seven seconds, and he was certainly well adrift of the field when he set off in pursuit of his rivals with only a lap and a half to go. But he reeled the rest in well before the finish, and won in 4min 4.2sec. The incident with Clarke is memorialised in a sculpture, entitled *Sportsmanship*, by Mitch Mitchell, which stands at the entrance to Olympic Park, Melbourne. According to journalist Harry Gordon, rather like Clarke's complaint that he is best known for his burned tee-shirt, while lighting the Olympic flame later that year, Landy is similarly rueful (or embarrassed) that he is remembered for that selfless act rather than his world Mile record. But for Clarke, it is all of a piece. "Landy is to me the equal of Elliott, but because Elliott won in an Olympic Games and Landy didn't - Landy's peak was after the Olympics - Elliott is put on a high pedestal, more than Landy. I wouldn't do that. Landy's career lasted for longer, he set the world record, he had as good a competition record. It's just that Herb's best race coincided with the Olympic Games, John's didn't. So what?"

'Crackpot,' 'pseudo-Nietzschean' or not, there is a lot of good sense in Cerutty's book, *Athletics*, and that Clarke should have a philosophy to expound is largely due to Cerutty having provided a framework to criticise. When the even more famous New Zealand coach, Arthur Lydiard came along immediately afterwards, and his trainee Peter Snell won three Olympic golds, it only emphasised that the nexus of middle and long distance excellence in that post-Zátopek decade had shifted to Australasia. Despite Clarke and Landy's ideological differences with Cerutty, there was one thing they could all agree on, and that was the significance of Zátopek. Cerutty was instrumental in setting up an annual 10,000 metres race in Australia, dedicated to Zátopek. Clarke's first world records came in the event. My colleague Len Johnson, who writes principally for *The Age* newspaper in Melbourne sent me this overview of an event inaugurated over 55 years ago, which only adds to Clarke's encomiums on Zátopek, and further highlights the enduring appeal of the Czech in Australia.

The Emil Zátopek 10,000 metres is one of the longest, continually run, track distance races in the world. Inaugurated in 1961 as the championship of the Victorian Marathon Club (which was) formed in 1946, with Percy Cerutty as its first president, the VMC was about more than just marathons.... Ron Clarke won the first three races (and five in all), setting the first of many world records in 1963 with new marks for Six Miles and 10,000 metres. From Clarke to Craig Mottram, via Steve Moneghetti, with Lisa Ondieki and Eloise Wellings, pretty well every significant Australian distance runner has won the Zátopek: 10, as it is now styled. The only tangible reward to the winner, however, is a rudimentary trophy hewn from a red-gum railway sleeper.... "Solid, tough and durable," (Les) Perry wrote of the trophy, "as appropriate to such an event, and to perpetuate the name and contribution to world and Olympic sport by this greatest of all distance runners".

It is fitting that Clarke's five victories in the 'Zátopek: 10' remain a record. And it was enormously gratifying to hear a champion - Clarke himself set close to a score of world records - be so complimentary, endearing and appreciative of an historical rival. Clarke admitted that he never tired of talking about Zátopek and the example he set. And in defence of Clarke's view that gold medals are far from being the greatest arbiter of excellence, I would venture that Billy Mills and Lachie Stewart, who beat Clarke to Olympic and Commonwealth 10,000 metres gold in, respectively Tokyo 1964 and Edinburgh 1970, barely register on the Richter Scale of long-distance running achievement, whereas Clarke's world records during a career spanning a decade put him in the pantheon of all-time greats, alongside Kohlemainen, Nurmi, Gebrselassie and, naturally Emil Zátopek. Clarke, of course preferred to talk about Zátopek.

"I've never met anybody like Emil Zátopek, I'll repeat it a thousand times.

reakthrough! Emil, en route to victory in the World University Games 5000 metres in Paris 1947. He won the 1500 metres the previous day *(Hulton Archive – Getty Images)*

**ČESKOSLOVENSKO - MISTŘI SVĚTA V CROSS COUNTRY 10KM - HANNOVER 1947
JINDRA ROUDNÝ*LAĎA KOŘÁN*EMIL ZÁTOPEK*LUBOŠ VOMÁČKA* K.ZABLOUDIL**

Three of my principal interviewees; from left, Jindra Roudný, Laďa Kořán and Emil, who won the World Military cross country in Hanover 1947. The Czechoslovakia squad took the team title *(L Kořán)*

Emil's parents, Agneška and František in front of his birthplace in Kopřivnice *(CTK Photo)*

Emil on the way to his first
Olympic gold, the 10,000
metres in London 1948
(CTK Photo)

Emil's first two world records
were set at 10,000 metres,
both in Ostrava 1949

Dana and Emil, on the way home from training.

His greatest race: the 5000 metres at the
Olympic Games, Helsinki 1952 *(ullstein bild – Getty Images)*

Entering the Olympic stadium, to win the marathon, Helsinki 1952 *(CTK Photo)*

The most famous kiss in Olympic history *(Popperfoto – Getty Images)*

Family affair – four Olympic golds, 1952.

The shopping run, Prague 1952.

Gunning for Gunder! Hägg and Zátopek, the first two men under 14min for 5000m.

68: Soviet tanks behind, exile ahead!

Spurned at home, but fêted at the Munich Olympics 1972
Zátopek and peerless gymnast Věra Čáslavská. *(Bertram - Getty Images)*

Dana and Emil finally
relaxing at home
(Miroslav Zajíc – Getty Images)

I think the closest is John Landy, and Les Perry. They're both of the same pure character. But Zata was someone who was absolutely and completely special in his influence. I've already said why Australian athletics was so strong here. He was the grandfather of our athletics, really, because of his influence with Les Perry. I think it went right through the sport. It took a long time, but the other people in the world that said you shouldn't compete very often, and that you shouldn't talk to the opposition; all that sort of stuff got back into vogue.

"Emil was the absolute antithesis of that. He talked to everybody, helped everybody. He trained everybody, gave them training secrets. 'What's training secrets?' You have to train, what's the big deal? He would help anybody. Anybody who went to him always had a story about how Emil helped them. Talk to Dave Stephens, talk to Mimoun. Mimoun's story? Forget about winning the ('56 Olympic) marathon. Mimoun's story was, when he finished the marathon, he just wanted to see Emil, and Emil came in fifth or sixth, and he raced up to Emil and said, 'My friend, I won, I won. I won the race. And he said, my greatest moment was when Emil stood to attention and saluted him. And he said, that was my greatest moment in sport – not breaking the tape, not being acclaimed by the crowd, but Emil Zátopek acclaiming him. That was his great moment. And that's the way Emil Zátopek affected everybody who knew him.

"The stories I tell are of Emil and, I suppose, John Landy to a certain extent. Because I think that both of them exemplify the spirit of what competition's all about, what sport's all about, what life's all about, to be even more serious about it all. About living and let-living, and helping other people seemed to me to be a good game; and these guys typified, epitomised it. I can't say enough. He was an enthusiast. I believe he was the biggest driving force and influence that athletics has ever seen".

40.

I'm glad I didn't make a special trip from Prague to visit the Zátopek Museum in Emil's birthplace of Kopřivnice. As a quid-pro-quo for the help that Carlo Capalbo and his team at the Prague Marathon were giving me, I went to one of their promotions in Olomouc, to do some online television commentary on the half-marathon in the town. Olomouc is only an hour's drive from Kopřivnice, rather than the four or five hours it would have taken from Prague. And frankly, the museum was a disappointment. It was an adjunct to the Tatra Motor Museum, and there was no indication outside the building that there was anything there concerning the Zátopeks. The student who chauffeured us to Kopřivnice was from that area, and didn't know of the Zátopek annexe. Nor, it turned out did his mother, and she was a local councillor in an adjacent town. That was a clear enough indication of the significance of the exhibition, which was a one-room collection of artefacts, statuettes, medals, pictures and a video-loop of Olympic footage, all lit with garish pink and purple lighting.

The motor museum was much more interesting, and a reminder yet again of how the Czechoslovak lands had been the workshop of the Austro-Hungarian Empire. Initially an engineering company created in 1850, Tatra started producing motor vehicles in 1897, making it the third oldest car company in the world (after Daimler and Peugeot). The company still produces trucks, and a Tatra 815 won Paris-Dakar six times in succession at the turn of the century. And the museum features a fine collection, going right back to the 19th century, dozens of models, of cars, trucks, even planes.

But, from the Zátopek perspective, it was a chance comment that saved the day. As we were leaving to go and visit Emil's birthplace a couple of streets away, one of the museum receptionists said, "Next time, you should visit the place where he is buried". We had been thinking of travelling on to Zlín, to see what remained of the celebrated Bata shoe factory, where the teenage Zátopek had worked during his formative years, and where he had begun his running career. But that round-trip would have taken several hours, and in any case, I would be going there on my next Czech trip some weeks later, when I visited Jindřich Roudný, Zátopek's oldest surviving training partner. So after visiting the non-descript suburban house, sporting its new plaque designating it as Zátopek's birthplace, we decided to carry on the extra hour into the mountains, to visit his grave in Rožnov pod Radhoštěm. That was well worth the detour.

Prior to the development of the Wallachian Open Air Museum, where Emil and many other Moravian dignitaries – poets, writers, musicians, sports stars – have memorial stones, Rožnov was probably best known as being where tennis star Martina Hingis spent her childhood. The museum is modelled on Scandinavia *skansen*, sites where old wooden buildings are collected from the surrounding area, and reconstructed to form a village. And indeed, a sign outside indicated that the Norwegian arts council had helped fund the museum. The centrepiece of the village (there are also separate restaurants and mills) is an impressive wooden church, surrounded by a metre high hedge, barely three to four metres from the walls. There are no graves, simply memorial stones nestling at the foot of the hedge, and Dana later told me that Emil had chosen the site because, two years prior to his death, the Olympic champion discus thrower, Ludvík Daněk was one of the first sports celebrities to have a stone there, as later was the Olympic champion ski-jumper Jiří Raška, whose family lived in Rožnov. Raška, by the way was another signatory of the *2000 Words Manifesto*.

The fields behind the Zátopek home in Kopřivnice reminded me of the industrial village where I grew up and began running. That was in the early 1960s, when running was an esoteric pursuit, and runners subject to derision in the street. Twenty years prior to that, Zátopek would not even run on his rare visits home from the Bata factory or the army barracks. Even when he was an established international track star, he still remembered his family saying that he would embarrass them if he ran in the town. Nowadays, Kopřivnice is doubtless like my own home village. When I paid a visit to a running club friend in the Black Country a couple of years ago, he complained that where once he knew everyone who ran past his house, now he knew no one, "but there are hordes of 'em".

The big difference and it is a subject which provokes much debate and dismay in the running community, is that worthy as it to keep fit and set personal targets, such as running a marathon inside four hours, none of these joggers will ever be a track star, because they don't know how to train hard enough to hurt themselves. It is one of the curiosities of running training, or indeed any effort, that what seems like fatigue is more often the body trying to trick the mind into giving up. The family friend, former decathlete and leading Czech journalist, Štěpán Škorpil told me he once asked Emil how he could possibly cope with running one hundred times 400 metres at speed, with only a short interval of jogging between efforts. "He said," reported Škorpil, "When I get to seventy, I just say to myself, only 30 more, then eighty, 20 more, ninety, ten more".

41.

Shortly after Kon Ichikawa's *Tokyo Olympiad* went on general release in the UK, in 1965, I went to the Odeon in Dudley, to enjoy what has proven to be the best Olympic film after Leni Reifenstahl's *Olympia*, itself a groundbreaking piece of cinema, marred only by its fascist overtones and casual racism (cuts from kangaroos hopping in Berlin Zoo, to black athletes in bounding practice). The Tokyo film had originally been destined for the great Japanese director Akira Kurosawa whose *Seven Samurai*, among many other works, is considered one of the seminal movies in cinema history. When Kurosawa failed to get complete control of the finished product he resigned the commission and Ichikawa stepped in. He took a very different route to Reifenstahl who concentrated on a grandiose Olympic overview along with some innovative camera work which has defined television sports coverage ever since. Ichikawa on the other hand pursued a far more accessible and humanistic path, following a half dozen personalities in some of the most prominent events in the 1964 Games. I still vividly recall the tears (of shame, indignity?) of the Japanese judo-player Akio Kaminaga after he had lost in the Open final to the giant Dutchman Anton Geesink, who had previously become the first non-Japanese to win a world title.

But the main attraction for myself and a crowd of pals from Tipton Harriers, sitting in front of me was the marathon, and the lengthy sequences dominated by the immortal Abebe, the Ethiopian who, four years earlier had won the first Olympic athletics gold by an African athlete, and had done so in totemic fashion. The unheralded Ethiopian began his sprint to victory in Rome 1960 at the obelisk looted from the northern Ethiopian city of Axum by Mussolini's troops over two decades before. Abebe would become the first man to win successive Olympic marathons. But one of the highlights for myself and the Tipton boys was the follow-up to Abebe's entry into the Tokyo Olympic Stadium. All of four minutes later came the Japanese, Kōkichi Tsuburaya*, but hard on his heels (and flying) was a guy we all knew – Basil Heatley from the splendidly named Coventry Godiva Harriers, on the other side of Birmingham.

The lads couldn't restrain themselves, and broke into spontaneous applause and cheers, with cries of, 'C'mon Bas!'

Heatley is described in most athletics reference books as a marathon runner, doubtless by dint of his Olympic silver in Tokyo (he flew past Tsuburaya in the finishing straight), and his marathon world record earlier in the year in the then celebrated Polytechnic Marathon, the original London marathon. But to us, Basil was a peerless cross country runner. We all ran in the Birmingham Cross Country League, then, I would venture the strongest competition in the world. What we admired about Basil was not only his self-effacing excellence – he won dozens of Division One races, in addition to national victories and the international title (prelude to the world championship) – but sometimes, in preparation for big races, he was happy to 'jog' around a league race in 10th or 12th place, ensuring team points. In short, Basil was a local hero, writ large.

Basil worked in local government and when, following retirement from elite racing, he got a job in Dudley in the mid seventies, he joined our local club, and continued to trot around Third Division races to make up the numbers, oblivious to what others might see as the mighty fallen. He also gave back to the grass roots by serving for decades as an official and race marshal for the Midland Counties AAA. Although I left the midlands around that time, I did get to meet him properly and talk about his experiences – in the past, we wouldn't have dared to approach such a celebrity – and the one thing he was adamant about was that he saw no merit whatsoever in an Olympic silver medal, awarded for finishing four minutes behind the winner, even if it was Abebe.

In mid-2015, after Colin Kirkham, an old sparring partner of mine, and a Coventry club-mate of Heatley's heard my *BBC* radio programme on Zátopek, he got in touch to say I should talk to Basil, since he was a Zátopek devotee. When I had finished my latest round of research, I gave Heatley a call – he had since moved back to the east midlands – and he was just as accessible as he had been years before. But one thing had changed; he had finally come to terms with that Olympic defeat. "Truly, it took me over 40 years to turn it round. From being negative, thinking how on earth can I take acclaim when I've been whupped by four minutes? Then only in recent years have I stopped to think, well, all the rest of the world had the opportunity to close him down, and they couldn't. Let's just accept that he was an extraordinary distance runner".

Heatley had finished no closer to Zátopek in his only encounter with one of the Olympic marathon champions prior to Abebe. That was in a cross country race in San Sebastian, in Spain's Basque country in 1958. It was Zátopek's last race. But, in common with Czech journalist Štěpán Škorpil, who said he 'met' Zátopek in 1952 via the radio, Heatley said, "My first encounter with Emil? I've just gone to my bookshelf, and I've got a book entitled, *Zátopek, The Marathon Victor*, by František Kožík. That was bought for me in 1955, by a little man I met when I was in the army, stationed at Melton Mowbray, and in many ways I seemed to have known Emil Zátopek since then, because it was, for better or worse, my bible. Another book I've got on Zátopek is by Bob Phillips, written about 12 years ago, and it got me motivated again (he was 70 at the time). I got it when it first came out. I'd already had both Achilles' tendons stripped years ago, and going out again just caused the problem to flare up again. So I put the book away, and haven't looked at it again until now. The first book, I was reading it when I was 22, 23, 24, it gets you going...

"I first met up with him in San Sebastian in 1958, the end of January. A great bloke! He won the race, I was about 10th or 12th; and we ended up with exactly the same prize, because for first prize, they'd got a double-barrelled shotgun, and tried to give it to him, but he wouldn't go anywhere near it. No, no, no, he said, I'll have one of these, and reached down the line and picked up a wristwatch; and I chose exactly the same. But, wonderful bloke. His English was good. I remember, once upon a time, I might have heard it or read it, somebody described him as looking like an aged peasant; and I thought, yeah, that'll do me. He was just an ordinary, relaxed character, who liked talking to people. I've got a story, I might have read it, I don't know, but I've always believed that Zátopek told me this...... early in '52, the Czech coaches went to him, remembering who Zátopek was and could virtually do as he liked. Anyway, they said, look Emil, you've been great, your training has stood you in good stead, but the world is catching you up, you're not training fast enough. Oh yes, I am, he said, I've got to get fitter and stronger, strength will prevail in the end. No, you've got to do some faster work; otherwise they'll stay with you and beat you on the run-in. No, he said, let me do it my way. He did it his way, and he went home with three gold medals…

"And I took that as my mantra. I've got to do 24 (six miles) or 25 laps (10,000m), to gain a little bit each lap, and then if I'm far enough away, it doesn't matter how fast they run. In hindsight, because the Czech coaches were probably right, what I was doing, I was training very hard for 10k, but actually doing exactly what was right for a marathon. It came good at the end…. I used to do 20 times a quarter(-mile), around 60 (secs) with half laps in between; and I'd run two, three miles from my home up to Bedworth to do that, and I would have run home from work in Coventry before that. So it added up to a fair bit. Then I'd come home and look at Zatopek running through the snow in his boots; which, of course Roy Fowler did, and I did once or twice, but it wasn't a clever thing to do…"

Zátopek may have side-stepped the prize shotgun, but after being fêted in the streets and bars of San Sebastian after his victory, he had a present thrust on him that he couldn't refuse, one which seemed to cause endless pleasure, both to him and Dana, and their many friends and training aquaintances back home. 'The Basques carried me around on their shoulders, tossed their traditional leather wine sacks at me and were generally thrilled by my success. Out on the streets of San Sebastian, people were coming up and hugging me, inviting me for a drink, and bringing gifts. The biggest surprise came when one guy opened a box containing a little white dog. I tried my hardest to avoid taking the gift, but in vain! He brought it to the train, and so I was occupied for the whole journey back home. I had to feed it, keep it warm, but mostly hide it from the ticket collectors; it was the same in the train, in the hotel in Paris, and also on the plane to Prague. He put up with everything, and in the end we gave him the fine Spanish name, Pedro. We couldn't go anywhere without him because everyone liked him so much. The kids from the whole house were coming to borrow him for playing. The stadium became his second home. He was running around there, but only with Dana, because I stopped racing after San Sebastian'.

* Tsuburaya's death, by suicide, four years later is one of the saddest stories in athletics history. Feeling that he had humiliated himself and dishonoured his

nation by being passed by Heatley in the finishing stages inside the Olympic stadium, he vowed to train harder, and win the marathon in Mexico 1968. Acute lumbago and other injuries meant that he failed to qualify for Mexico. He committed ritual suicide in early 1968, leaving a note for his parents, which began, 'Cannot run anymore...'.

42.

Zátopek's World Records

5000 metres	13min 57.2sec	Colombes, Paris	May 30, 1954
Six Miles	28:08.4	Stará Boleslav	Nov 1, 1953
	27:59.2	Brussels	June 1, 1954
10,000 metres	29:28.2	Ostrava	June 11, 1949
	29:21.2	Ostrava	Oct 22, 1949
	29:02.6	Turku, Finland	August 4, 1950
	29:01.6	Stará Boleslav	November 1, 1953
	28:54.2	Trois Tilleuls, Brussels	June 1, 1954
10 Miles	48:12.0	Stará Boleslav	Sept 29, 1951
20,000 metres	1hr 01min 15.8sec	Strahov, Prague	Sept 15, 1951
	59:51.8	Stará Boleslav	Sept 29, 1951
15 Miles	1:16:26.4	Stará Boleslav	Oct 26, 1952
	1:14:01.0	Celákovice	Oct 29, 1955
25,000 metres	1:19:11.8	Stará Boleslav	Oct 26, 1952
	1:16:36.4	Celákovice	Oct 29, 1955
30,000 metres	1:35:23.8	Stará Boleslav	Oct 26, 1952
One Hour Run	19,558 metres	Strahov, Prague	Sept 15, 1951
	20,052 metres	Stará Boleslav	Sept 29, 1951

Zátopek's Medals

Gold – Olympic Games, London 1948 – 10,000 metres
      Olympic Games, Helsinki 1952 – 5000/10,000 metres/Marathon
      European Championships, Brussels 1950 – 5000/10,000 metres
      European Championships, Berne 1954 – 10,000 metres
Silver – Olympic Games, London 1948 – 5000 metres
Bronze – European Championships, Berne 1954 – 5000 metres

43.

Late one Saturday afternoon in midsummer 2015, I was preparing to go for a run in Stromovka when I heard an email ping into my inbox. Slave to the internet, I only hesitated briefly, with my hand on the door, before going over to the computer to check - and stared, uncomprehendingly at the subject line. 'Zane Branson, RIP'. My first impulse was denial - this must be Zane sending news from Kenya of the death of one of his or another manager's athletes. But no, this was an email from David Monti, a New York running buff, who had heard of Zane's heart attack from friends in Iten, where Zane had been staying for several days, visiting and planning with his new partner, his colleagues and roster of athletes.

I slumped into the chair, and unable to find Zane's deputy, Davor's phone number, I emailed him. He replied straightaway. I called to hear the tragic account of Zane's death that morning, one of the saddest aspects of which was that he had gone on the African trip with his new partner. For the two months prior to that trip, I had not seen him happier in the 20 years I had known him. I stared into space for a long time then went for my run. I would have gone for a run anyway, since it seemed the only sensible thing to do, to trace the path through Stromovka that I'd taken with Zane on one of his own rare training runs a couple of months before. After I got back and showered, I headed for the Café Spitfire, the bar that Zane had introduced me to some months before. There, I wrote an obituary, which I posted on my website that night.

Zane Branson who, among many other things was a runner, an athlete-manager, and a friend has died, aged 57, of a suspected heart attack in Iten, Kenya on Saturday, July 25.

To many people in the athletics business, 'athlete-manager' is a term of abuse, belonging in those nether regions infested by politicians, corporate bankers and second-hand car salesmen. But Zane elevated the term to a stratosphere few could aspire to. As a manager, he was solicitous to a fault.

I particularly recall an incident around 15 years ago. I arrived at a post-race party for the Belgrade Marathon, an event that we both worked on for many years. Questioning his absence, it turned out that one of the Kenyan runners had collapsed, and Zane had taken him to hospital. Despite assurances that all the runner needed was re-hydration, rest and a good night's sleep, Zane stayed at his bedside all night. This was before Zane was a full-time manager, but he had helped recruit the runner, and felt responsible. That was typical Zane behaviour.

More recently, he told me about an ageing father of one of his Kenyan athletes, who had cycled around 100 kilometres (60 miles), to thank Zane personally for the help he had given to his son. That meant far more to Zane than ten per cent.

As long-time friend and business associate, Davor Savija wrote earlier today, "Zane was a man with a fine touch and attention to detail; and he was fully and completely devoted to athletes, and not only to the athletes he worked with. Athlete Management in East Africa was not only a business for Zane, it was a calling and a platform for a rich life, sacrifice and dreams".

Zane was a private person; he rarely volunteered information about his life. But piecing together stray comments and info from other sources, it seems that Zane enjoyed several lives. Born in Ohio in 1957, I understand the family (ironically, long-lived) moved to West Virginia, where they still own a farm. As a late teenage runner, he took part in the relay from the White House to Montreal prior to the Olympic Games in 1976. I think he slept rough once he got there, but he was more impressed by hanging out at the training track, and watching the likes of John Walker and other luminaries going through their paces.

He attended East Tennessee State University, where he was a team mate of a largely Irish contingent of runners, headed by Ray Flynn. Ray wrote tonight, "Zane was passionate for running from the time I first met him at East Tennessee State University, where he was one of the top runners. He made friends wherever he went and will be sorely missed in the Athletics World".

Zane's major claim to (almost) running fame came in the Kay-Pro 10k in 1984. The computer company organised a national-wide State-based race for athletes who had never won a major competition. The male and female winners were due to receive an unprecedented $500,000 each. Zane won the Tennessee race, and (only the winners) went forward to the final in Las Vegas, where he was leading until the last kilometre when, as he told me recently, "I suddenly couldn't breathe, it was the only time it ever happened to me". He finished second, but it turned out that the half a million bucks to the winners was to be paid out at $10,000 per year for 50 years. The company went bust two years later; so Zane didn't feel so bad at only picking up an early computer, which he sold for a thousand dollars.

Zane was a big fan of the blues, and was involved in music management for a long time, working on gigs with giants like Fats Domino and Van Morrison, James Brown and Chuck Berry, and guys I'd never heard of. When he came to live in Liverpool 30 years ago, through the auspices of Gerry Helme, second in the London Marathon in the early eighties, he helped organise gigs in Liverpool and Manchester, while also working in his degree subject, Health and Hospital Management.

He and Gerry started a minor athletics management company, and a chance meeting with them in 1992 resulted in me, then a full-time journalist, branching out into setting up a marathon media service. On the music front, when I had a BIG birthday, Zane arranged for the Rock 'n' Roll band ('fraid so), who ushered in my second half-century.

I am writing this in a bar in Prague, a bar that Zane recommended to me a year ago, saying, "It's got good music, not too loud, so you can hold a conversation; and there's some nice folk go there". Amen to that!

When I leave here, I'm going back to Zane's flat. He has a base here because, despite being a long-time resident of Belgrade, the Czech Republic has the advantage of being in the Schengen area; and since his business, the International Athletics Consultancy has flourished, the location affords easier travel across Europe for his athletes, among whom the major names include Patrick Makau, Emily Chebet, Joyce Chepkirui and Wilson Chebet. Zane was also instrumental is setting up the RunCzech Running Team for Carlo Capalbo, race director of the Prague International Marathon.

When I told Zane a year ago that I was going to research a project on Emil Zátopek, he just gave me a set of keys to his flat, refusing, inevitably to accept any recompense.

He spent several days in Addis Ababa, talking with his Ethiopian athletes and other contacts, before going to Kenya around ten days ago. According to his partner Evgeniya, he experienced some chest pains in Addis, but they disappeared after two days, and he thought he might get a check-up in Kenya.

Business partner, Savija said, "Zane was walking from the police station towards Iten town. He was with our French-born, Kenya-based associate, Julien Di Maria (known by his pseudonym Kip Evans). They were due to meet with the Wilson Chebet group, and watch their 40k long run. As he walked with Julien, they were joking, brainstorming and planning. Suddenly, Zane turned towards Julien and collapsed. He was admitted to Iten District Hospital but he was not responsive, neither breathing, nor was there any pulse. Doctors did their best with limited resources".

There are not too many people in the world like Zane Branson; and our poor little planet, situated somewhere on the hinterland of the vast expanse of the Milky Way is today a sadder place for his demise.

Zane Edward Branson was born on September 23, 1957, in Ohio, USA. He died on July 25, 2015, in Iten, Kenya.

Zane was buried in Iten.

44.

Although Emil retired, one is tempted to say, knackered, in 1958, Dana's career continued through to the Olympic Games in Rome 1960. In the years after her Olympic victory in 1952, she twice won the European title, in 1954 and 1958, and became the oldest woman to set a world record in the javelin when she threw 55.73 metres at home in Strahov Stadium, Prague, just short of her 36th birthday. Two years later, she was never close to winning in Rome but, again, just over two weeks short of her 38th birthday, she became the oldest Olympic medallist in the javelin when she outdid herself by adding silver to her gold medal of eight years earlier. Family friend and TV journalist Štěpán Škorpil remembered Dana's post-Rome satisfaction at having finally one-upped her celebrated partner. "He (Emil) was number one for everyone in the country, not just the people who like sport, but for everyone in the factories, in the offices.... if Emil was going for a discussion at a factory or at a school, there was no work done, it was 'Emil, our Emil'. Every time, Dana was one step behind, it was 'Emil, and his wife'. But after Rome 1960, they return in south Moravia, where Dana grew up, there was a big reception, and Dana used to say, 'for me it was absolutely super, because the commentator said, 'We welcome two-time Olympic medallist, Dana Zátopková.... and her husband'."

It was clear to everyone who knew them or saw them, particularly at schools events, that both Dana and Emil loved children. I took the precaution of asking Škorpil why they'd never had any of their own. "It's a secret room," he replied. "Because I have information... every time, Dana would say, when she was a competitor it's impossible to combine with motherhood, but about Stockholm 1958 (European Championships), I don't know, there was a rumour that she was pregnant. But I don't know if she had health problems. Then after Rome, she was 38, and in this time, it was impossible (to have) the first children above 40. Now it is common, but 50 years ago, when a woman was married at 23, 24, and didn't have a child, it wasn't normal".

After their retirement, they still travelled abroad, but to coach rather than compete. Emil told me how much he enjoyed a year coaching in Indonesia, in

1963, "but I never found any champions". Dana also spent six months there with him before returning to secure her position as national women's coach, a post she would hold for the next thirty years, even through the period of Emil's exile from Prague, although, as she said, "I had to fight to keep the position, but I had a lot of friends and allies".

However, in the years prior to the upheavals of 1968, Emil continued to accept invitations as guest of honour, including to the Olympic Games in Tokyo in 1964, where he met Ron Clarke for the first time; and in 1966 to Olympia itself, site of the Ancient Games, where Jean Durry, curator of the French national sports museum was also participating in a seminar at the Olympic Academy. In *Le Terrassier de Prague*, Pierre Naudin quotes Durry as saying he went for a jog in the original Olympic Stadium with Zátopek. 'It was one of the greatest experiences of my life. Zátopek chatted and joked, comparing ancient athletes with his own contemporaries. I listened, rapt by his intelligence and simplicity. And I'll always remember with what gravity he stretched out his foot to touch the grooves in the stone which the runners used as starting blocks. He cited several names of ancient athletes, and said quietly, Sport made them immortal'.

45.

Ron Clarke had another, very good reason to admire Emil Zátopek. It was occasioned by a visit to Prague later in 1966. When I met Zátopek in 1998, he told me that the Czechoslovak athletics federation had pressured him to invite Clarke to compete in Prague. It was a good job they did, because as Clarke said, "When I was touring, I didn't like competing in Iron Curtain countries, 'cause at that time, they were very stereotyped as to when they fed you; for example, they'd take you and feed you an hour before the race, that sort of stuff. But Emil invited me, and asked if I'd compete in Prague for him. Of course, I said, yeah, no problem". As it turned out, Clarke barely got to eat before the race anyway, since his plane was late, and he made do with a couple of bananas that Emil - who had picked him up at the airport - just happened to have in his car. Since Emil had long since retired, there was no Czechoslovak distance runner who could finish within minutes of Clarke, even at his lesser distance of 5000 metres, so a compromise was reached, with Josef Odložíl, Olympic 1500 metres silver medallist two years earlier in Tokyo, being persuaded to race Clarke at 3000 metres.

Clarke had some doubts himself, fearing it would be 'the same old story,' he'd lead throughout the race, and the miler Odložíl would outsprint him at the end. But Emil 'coached' Ron to run a few rapid sprints before the race, which apparently made a big impression on the watching Odložíl, who didn't respond when Clarke put in a mid-race surge. Clarke said, "Emil barracked for me right through the race, and told me how far I was ahead of Josef. See, he hated 'sitters', so he always barracked for the distance runners against the sitters, didn't matter where they came from". Clarke stayed with the Zátopeks and the following morning made the pilgrimage to Houšťka stadium in Stará Boleslav, where Emil had set the trio of world records in 1952. They went for a run together in the surrounding woods. Emil told Ron that he was far from fit, but Ron reported that it was, "the hardest run I'd had in several weeks". They drove the 30 kilometres back home for lunch before Emil took... well, let Ron tell the story....

"He said you must get some crystal before you go back. He was in mufti, and he was usually stationed out of Prague in those days, in 1966. So we pulled up in the main street, and we went in and we came out, and here's a policeman giving him a ticket. Emil gets within 20 metres of him, and he wakes up to the fact that it's Emil's car. And his face lights up, and he tears up the ticket, turns it around and Emil signs it. Emil jumps in, because we didn't find any decent crystal in the place we were in, he does a U-turn in front of him, and everyone screeches to a stop. He reckons he's sacred or something; and he went past another traffic station with a guy in the middle, and there's another guy on the pedestrian side, leading the pedestrians. It was getting very close to lunchtime by this time, it was very busy, and he parked again, obviously where you can't park, and the guy in the middle blew his whistle and waved him on, and the guy standing next to him looked around and waved him on. Emil waved back at them, and got out of the car. So this guy went red, being defied, and came tearing up to him and, again, gets within about 15 metres and sees Emil Zátopek and, ah, he can't believe it, races up to him and shakes him by the hand…. animated conversation. We go in the shop, I get worried and worried, it's a nice shop, I kept on saying, Emil, what about your car? 'No problem, no problem'. We come out, and the car's disappeared, it's gone!

"So Emil does this whistle that I can't do, but he could whistle between his teeth, so he does this huge whistle, and the policeman, who parked his car for him, gets back in the car, drives it back, does the U-turn, and shakes him by the hand, and goes. So my - I tell this story as often as I can – my definition of fame is when a policeman will go and park the car for you while you shop in the middle of a busy weekday lunchtime peak period. That is fame! And no football star ever gets that treatment in this country. And Emil Zátopek was someone special, and that was the sort of personality he was. He was fantastic.

"After this shopping episode, Emil had taken me around, and again taken me through customs, like when he met me off the plane; so through customs we go and straight to the plane, forget about paying duty on the crystal vase I had. He got me on the plane, and said thanks for coming, I loved your visit, and as he shook my hand on the top of the plane steps, he said this is for you, you deserve it. It was a little package. I thought I was smuggling something out of the country for him, so I put it in my pocket, and pretended I didn't get it, and didn't open it or anything. Again, knowing the Iron Curtain countries, and how hard it was to take goods in and out of the country, currency and so on, I thought it must have some secret instructions I had to do for him. So I was going to wait until I got through the customs in England, but as we landed in London, curiosity overcame me, so I thought I'd better look before the customs, because they'll ask me what it's about when they see it. So I opened it up, and here's his gold medal. He's given me his gold medal from '52..."

46.

The movement known as the Prague Spring*, the period of liberalisation following the forced resignation of Antonin Novotný as First Secretary and President, and his replacement by Alexander Dubček and Ludvik Svoboda had all the more impact since it was concurrent with the 20th anniversary of 'Victorious February', the parliamentary coup of 1948 which had ushered in hard-line Communism. In 1968, Dubček's promises of more freedom, of expression and travel among other things, were put to the test almost immediately by the Union of Czech Writers who took the gazette *Literání Noviny*, which had always followed the Party line, and made it truly independent. The name was changed to *Literání Listi*, and within months it was selling 300,000 copies, a figure which would provoke hot flushes among literary revue publishers across the world nowadays. In the flush of this new dawn, writer Ludvík Vaculík authored the document known as the *2000 Words Manifesto*. It was hardly revolutionary. It was more a plaint about remote government taking clandestine decisions which had led to a moral and economic decay. It avoided criticising Communism per se, and backed reformist elements in government, while underlining a need for social order.

The Soviet Union was not even mentioned, though there was reference to a potential corrective intervention. It was published on June 27, 1968 in four prominent journals, including two dailies, and its ultimate significance was that it had been made public completely independently of the Party. As prominent dissident Jan Urban told Czech Radio in 2008, on the 40th anniversary of the *2000 Words*, 'everything about this was saying 'We don't need the Communist party anymore. We can do things on our own'." The *2000 Words* was only endorsed by a few dozen people at the time, but their names were all significant; among them were four famous sports personalities, all Olympic champions – ski jumper Jiří Raška, peerless gymnast Věra Čáslavská, and the Zátopeks, Dana and Emil.

When I started working in the west midlands of the UK in the early 1960s it was common knowledge in engineering circles that pre-War Czechoslovakia had been one of the powerhouses of European industry. Being 'governed' after 1948 by the Soviet Union, which was still largely an agrarian economy, was hardly conducive to staying in the game economically. From being the 10th largest economy in the world in the 1930s, economic growth in Czechoslovakia in the early 1960s was the lowest even in eastern Europe.

In an interview in the early 90s, with Rich Benyo, editor of *Marathon & Beyond* magazine, Zátopek gave the view from the Czech street of how the country had suffered in the Soviet orbit. "It was the same problem as in Hungary 1956. When you have a lot of people in a country who cannot use their brains to help improve the country, for example in economics. It was always the same, if someone tried to propose something new, modern or better; 'No, it's not possible,' they were told. And if someone came with some criticism, they could go to prison, even our president of today, Václav Havel. When they said, we are having our emblem (slogan) 'The Truth Prevails', it was not true. When they were only speaking about human rights, it was not true. About democracy, it was not true. And anyone who protested went to prison.

'It was not possible because the Soviet Union was frightened. The Russian politicians were frightened. If Hungary were to be free, then Czech people want to be free, and if this danger of political separatism were to jump over the frontiers of the Soviet Union, then everyone would want to be free – Lithuania, Estonia, Ukraine. That's why they were so strong against; it was impossible to change something. If there was a strike or talk of democracy, it was very dangerous. I was in the army, and it was only possible to have official opinion, not private one".

* The Czechoslovaks themselves used the term 'Post-January Development' since it did not limit the activity to the capital city.

47.

At around 1am, on Wednesday, August 21, 1968, there was an unexpected announcement on Prague Radio.

'To the entire people of the Czechoslovak Socialist Republic, yesterday on August 20, at about 2300, troops of the Soviet Union, the Polish People's Republic, the German Democratic Republic, the Hungarian People's Republic and the Bulgarian People's Republic crossed the frontiers of the Czechoslovak Socialist Republic....'

The announcement went on to say that all of this happened not only with the full knowledge of the Czechoslovak Communist Party Central Committee, but that the said Committee had requested the intervention, and that the people should honour the request, and not offer any opposition.

The country was in the process of being invaded, and occupied.

It was not entirely unforeseen. Ludvik Vaculík had warned of the possibility in the *2000 Words Manifesto*. And those who were wondering why so many of the troops which had engaged in Warsaw Pact manoeuvres on the Czech borders just the previous month were still there, now had their answer.

After seven and a half months of Dubček's attempts at liberalisation, the Kremlin had had enough.

48.

Murray Sayle was one of those journalists who, in his heyday, in the nineteen sixties and seventies, was almost as famous as the people he wrote about. Among other accomplishments, he covered the Vietnam War from close quarters, climbed Everest, sailed the Atlantic solo, revealed that Che Guevara had joined Bolivian guerrillas, was the only man to interview the British double agent Kim Philby after his defection to Moscow, and quit UK journalism in infamous circumstances when the *Sunday Times* refused to publish his findings that British soldiers had deliberately fired on unarmed civilians in Northern Ireland on Bloody Sunday. Four years earlier, and typically, within hours of the Soviet-led invasion of Czechoslovakia in the early morning of August 21st, 1968, Sayle was on a plane to Vienna, whence he motored to the border, blagged his way through, and made his way to Prague.

In *AUGUST 21st: The Rape of Czechoslovakia*, authored by Colin Chapman, his foreign news editor at the *Sunday Times*, Sayle wrote about the extraordinary vituperation and resistance that virtually everyone in Czechoslovakia, save for a few quislings, were putting up against the invaders. Within a very short time, Sayle encountered the most famous man in the country. There were several clandestine radio stations, broadcasting defiance, but the Aussie journalist had been marvelling at the courage and ingenuity of television technicians and presenters who had set up 24 hour 'pirate' transmissions from a sequestered studio that the mighty Russian army could not find.

'I was as mystified as any Czech,' wrote Sayle, 'as to where these broadcasts were coming from and wondered how, in a country occupied by a powerful army, they were getting away with it. Some days later, Colonel Emil Zátopek, the Czech long-distance runner, let me into the secret. Zátopek, a national hero, continued a cheerful defiance throughout the occupation. He speaks a rapid if somewhat inaccurate English, and there is no doubt where he stands: "We were getting the socialism going really nice before these bloody Russians came". Zátopek, after removing the tabs of his rank to avoid compromising anyone, drove me to the Dum Hoteloveho Byleni apartment building in the suburb of Petriny, a half-finished block, twelve storeys high. The 'studio' was a kitchen in a flat on the twelfth floor.....

'... Zátopek, who is instantly recognised everywhere in Czechoslovakia, had been awakened by four Czechoslovak Army officers in the early hours of the 21st. "Have you come to take me with you, or take me away?" asked Zátopek. One of the officers replied, "Emil, the country needs your help". Zátopek spent the next four nights sleeping in different houses in Prague. On the Friday night, August 23rd, an Army officer drove him to the kitchen television studio, now decorated with its pictures of Svoboda (president) and Dubček (First Secretary).

'There he made his first underground broadcast, as one of the long list of Czech notables who by so appearing, established themselves in Russian eyes as determined counter-revolutionaries. By the second Sunday of the occupation, the Russians were reduced to systematically visiting every television transmitter to find where the mystery broadcasts were coming from. Somehow they discovered that programmes were coming from Bukova (the relay station), and they asked the staff at the Prague television headquarters where it was. There are three Bukovas in different parts of the country, and a large-scale map of Czechoslovakia is needed to find any of them. According to Zátopek, the Czech television men offered the Russians the best they could, a village called Bukovany, several hundred kilometres away. A detachment of Russian armoured-cars raced to Bukovany, and the astonished inhabitants had to submit to a totally inexplicable Russian search for a non-existent transmitter.

'The clandestine studio went off air on the Sunday of the Moscow agreement (a supposed compromise, two weeks after the invasion). "I am sure it was the television and radio which kept our people together," said Zátopek. "And as well, it was a hell of a lot of bloody fun".'

Sayle's account emphasises just how much Zátopek was right at the centre of resistance to the Russian invasion. For example, the incident where he berated the Soviet soldiers in Russian, telling them of the Ancient Olympic Truce – where battles in the Hellenic world were suspended for the duration of the Games – and asking what were they doing in Prague six weeks before the Mexico Olympics, became so famous that *Adidas* (he was one of their first sponsorees) made it the subject of a TV commercial in 1995.

That Zatopek made his feelings clear right from the start of the invasion is also evidenced by an interview he gave on August 26, five days after the tanks rolled in. A French film crew tracked him down to the physiotherapy department of a Prague hospital, and the footage can be found on the website of *l'INA, Institut national de l'audiovisuel.* Dressed in an army summer shirt sporting colonel's epaulettes, and massaging his left wrist, he begins by describing what could be read as a metaphor for his eventual situation. "I was on exercises with the battalion in Moravia, and I climbed a tree to pick some cherries. I fell down and broke my wrist. I had to have it in a cast, which has been off for two weeks now, but I'm here to get some rehabilitation on the wrist.

"At the moment I'm spending a lot of time in the streets, it's an interesting situation, and I'm very happy to do it. There are old people, intellectuals, workers, students, the whole nation is of the same opinion, that we have the right to live the way we want, with our own hopes and under our own sovereignty.... I work at the Ministry of Defence, and someone in the canteen asked me, what's it like in Moscow (where he had recently visited)? I told her, it's miserable. They don't understand. They're against democracy, against humanity, against everything. They're against progress in our country. Every nation wants the same liberty. And believe or not, the Russian people themselves want the same liberty. There is a big movement going on at the moment. This is the Year of Human Rights, it's also the year of the Olympic Games. It's the best opportunity to demonstrate this hope for liberty, for national self-determination, but all we're getting is the saddest demonstration of Russian fire-power."

This is the rhetoric he repeated time and time again to the crowds who would assemble to hear him give impromptu speeches in Wenceslas Square and elsewhere, sometimes to thousands of like-minded citizens, crowds pock-marked with the inevitable stooges and informers who were reporting back to the StB. Given that he made repeated calls, including to international media outlets for the Soviet Union to be excluded from the upcoming Olympic Games in Mexico, there would be no shortage of testimony to convict comrade Zátopek when the time came. It didn't happen immediately, but when the dust settled he would be one of the first and the most famous victim of 'normalizace', characteristic double-speak for the restoration of the dead-hand of Moscow-style centralised Communist control.

Long-time *BBC* foreign correspondent Martin Bell briefly enjoyed the same sort of fame as Murray Sayle, in the late 1990s. Bell covered many of the same conflicts as Sayle, and was wounded in action in Sarajevo during the disintegration of Yugoslavia. Bell decided to stand as an independent candidate for the UK Parliament in 1997, and turned over a 22,000+ Conservative majority in Tatton, Cheshire, against Neil Hamilton who had been involved in allegations of corruption. Bell won with his own landslide of over 11,000 votes. Close to 30 years earlier, he had done a seminal interview with Zátopek in Prague in early 1969, when it was becoming increasingly clear that the multiple Olympic champion and national hero was on the verge of being sanctioned severely for his opposition to the Soviet invasion. Bell, whose sartorial taste led to him being labelled the 'Man in the White Suit,' did the last radio interview that the White Knight would do for the next decade or two.

In the interview, Zátopek begins by describing his current situation, "..still I am in the army, I am Colonel in the Czechoslovak Army, and very popular sportsman from athletics history, but now it is very difficult for me. It is not allowed for me to speak to the people, not allowed to visit schools, not allowed to arrange my function in sports organisation... they ask (tell?) me always, you must not say any word. And I say, oh yes, I must not say anything, but the morning you leave (ban?) me from the function, and this evening, it will be broadcast in *BBC*, and in *(Radio) Free Europe*, and in *Voice of America*. Oh yes, you can forbid me everything, but people will see if I do not come to training, must not come to the children I am coaching now".

Bell ends by asking, "Do you think you're so popular that, in fact your position is safe?" Demonstrating the true nature of patriotism, Zátopek replies, "In this situation, it is not me who is in play. It is our future, our country, this democratic development, this humanity which we wanted to develop; and this is an unhappy situation".

49.

There was a period of détente after the Soviet led invasion of late August 1968. Dubček was taken immediately to Moscow, and returned several days later, sporting bruises on his face. There is an unparalleled account of the emotional radio speech he gave to the nation in Milan Kundera's *The Unbearable Lightness of Being*, a work in which Kundera demonstrates his mastery of seamlessly blending surrealist actuality with fiction and philosophical discourse. In the real world, Dubček was deposed as leader, although retaining the post of First Secretary for several months more. On the official front, little else happened publicly before spring 1969. The new hardliners, with Moscow's backing began dismantling Dubček's initiatives, preparing to replace them with the dead hand of 'normalisation'. If Dubček could be faulted, it would be in not seeing the consequences of his moves to liberalisation. He believed, wrongly that the Soviet urge for manipulation of its satellites had dimmed since the Hungarian invasion twelve years earlier. The ultimate humility was being posted as ambassador to Turkey later the following year, allegedly in the hope that he might defect.

That was probably the thinking behind the decision to permit Dana and Emil to accept the invitation of the Local Organising Committee, and attend the Games of the XIX Olympiad in Mexico City, six weeks after the invasion. And indeed, while in Mexico, the Zátopeks were offered sanctuary in Britain, Sweden and Finland, where the couple had so distinguished themselves at the Helsinki Olympics 16 years earlier. But, like Dubček, Dana and Emil turned down the opportunity to defect. As Dana said simply in 2014, "We did not want to leave our country".

If Emil and Dana had been the stars of the show in Helsinki 1952, it was a friend and colleague, and co-signatory of the 2000 word manifesto, Věra Čáslavská who was the *pièce de résistance*, in more ways than one at Mexico 1968. In the comparatively short history of Czechoslovakia, 1918-1993, she was the only Olympic sports celebrity* who can remotely compare with Zátopek in international esteem. Indeed the peerless gymnast won far more medals, gold or otherwise than Zátopek - seven Olympic golds and four silvers, four world titles, plus five silvers and a bronze; and no fewer than 11 European golds. In one heady period, 1964-68, spanning Tokyo and Mexico, her two Olympic Games, she won double the number titles of all the Soviet women gymnasts combined.

While she was a radiant personality on the bars, beams and mat, Čáslavská was a retiring person in public life. She did not seek the limelight. Just about the only public declaration she had made prior to signing the *2000 Words Manifesto* had been, coincidentally, a defence of Emil in a student magazine. She was not a natural actor like Zátopek. But where his public stance against the occupation came in the streets and on the pirate TV and radio stations of 'Occupied' Czechoslovakia, Čáslavská's repudiation of the Russians came in front of a TV audience of millions worldwide, in Mexico, where she not only won the hearts of the locals with her elegant victories, and her very public wedding (attended by thousands) to Tokyo silver medal runner Josef Odložil, but also ensured, like Zátopek had already done, her internal exile when she got back home.

As a signatory of the *2000 Words Manifesto*, she was already a marked woman, and her preparation for the Games had correspondingly been compromised. She was advised to get out of Prague for the six weeks prior to the Games, and famously completed her preparation by training on five-barred gates and bales of hay out in the countryside. Like the rest of the Czechoslovak Olympic squad, she only learned at the last minute that they would go to Mexico. But once there, she made her mark as indelibly as Tommie Smith and John Carlos.

In his biography *Věra Čáslavská, Life on Olympus*, political historian Pavel Kosatík writes, 'When Věra bumped into Russian athletes in the Olympic village they ignored each other. The atmosphere in the gymnastics auditorium surrounding the Czechoslovak and Soviet teams was so intense that Věra went on to say that it felt more like she was in a bullfighting ring than at the top gymnastics competition. But there was no doubt that it was Věra who the audience was cheering for. In Mexico, Věra had been declared the second most popular woman on the planet after Jackie Kennedy... huge political importance was now attached to sporting victories. Beating the Russians in sport was the only method of victory still available to the Czechoslovaks. By turning her head away from the Soviet flag, Věra could not have fulfilled this task any better'.

While their black-gloved raised hands at the 200 metres victory ceremony presaged Olympic exclusion, official vilification and reduced job opportunities for years for Smith and Carlos, Čáslavská's bowed head while the Soviet anthem played at two award ceremonies where she had 'only' won silver ensured decades of being a 'non-person' in her home country for the greatest gymnast in history. But she never recanted her stance, though offered work and reintegration to do so. In an interview with *BBC* in 2012, Čáslavská said, "I did everything in my power to defeat the Occupiers". TV commentator, Štěpán Škorpil recalls, "Věra Čáslavská was fantastic in Mexico, talking about the Occupation. And when the Czech team came into the stadium, everyone stood and applauded, shouting, 'Czecho, Czecho, Ra-Ra-Ra'. It was an electric atmosphere. It was one of the moments when Vera made herself 100% clear. She told me many times, the only idea in these competitions was to beat the Russians; not the French, German, Italians. It was, 'beat the Russians'."

In normal circumstances, Čáslavská would have been fêted when she returned home to Prague, given awards and the coaching post that she expected, even demanded on occasion. But in 'normalizace' circumstances, she was ostracised for the better part of two decades. Like Zátopek, the authorities reluctantly allowed her to go without spouse to the Olympic Games in Munich 1972 when, Kosatík records, she was centre screen on Czechoslovak TV on at least one occasion, with commentators remaining mute. Finally, in 1979, she was permitted to take up a coaching post in Mexico, where she was still idolised, but even that seemed to require pressure from the Mexicans over oil exports. She stayed two years, during which time her marriage to Odložil foundered, and they were divorced in the mid-1980s, almost concurrent with a visit to Prague by the IOC president Juan-Antonio Samaranch, who surprised his hosts by belying his own totalitarian background – he had been a supporter of the Franco dictatorship - and insisted on not only meeting Čáslavská and Zátopek publicly, but awarding them the Olympic Order.

Following the Velvet Revolution, when both she and Zátopek were restored to public life, she became one of only two women to join the inner-circle of playright-President Václav Havel at Hradcaný Castle. But her life was short-circuited again in 1993, when her ex-husband Josef and their son Martin got into a fight in a Prague nightclub, and Odložil père died from a head wound. Martin was jailed but got a reprieve from Havel four years later. Sections of the media blamed his pardon on favouritism, due to Čáslavská's fame and proximity to the President. She withdrew again from public life. Martin, in the meantime went to live in Ireland for several years, and I spotted his name, down the field in a couple of road races there during that period. I had hoped to interview Čáslavská personally, and spoke to her on the phone in late 2014. But she was already ill with pancreatic cancer, which necessitated a major operation in mid-2015, and she referred me to her biographer Kosatík.

* Apologies to the incomparable javelin thrower, Jan Železný, whose first of three Olympic golds (after a silver) came in 1992, just prior to the dissolution of the country. He also won three world titles representing the Czech Republic, and set an as yet unapproached world record. Now, I did share a beer with him one time, but that's another story...

50.

Lubo Šmatana, the Czech Radio reporter who had sent me the StB (secret police) files on Zátopek, told me that he could find nothing particularly condemnatory in them. 'From time to time, some journalists write that Zátopek collaborated with StB, but there is no evidence of it. Studying his opinions and positions shows he wasn't really interested in politics but (that) he had to (be)'. Nonetheless, there are reams and reams of inconsequential notes, proof that like with the infamous East German Stasi, being an StB agent must have been the most mind-numbing job in the world, even when following round or listening in to a volatile character like Zátopek, who was incapable of hiding his allegiances.

On that latter point, in a file labelled *648808_MV_1_2_0014_1*, and dated July 17, 1968 (five weeks before the Warsaw Pact invasion), there is a gloss on an interview Zátopek gave to the (pre-Murdoch) UK newspaper the Sun, which concludes, 'In another part of the interview, Zátopek talked about his travels around the world as an athlete during the Stalinist (sic) regime in Czechoslovakia. He said that he was sad wherever he went because he knew he was representing a bad government; apparently he never hid his feelings'.

In another file, dated November 9 (almost three months after the invasion, and after Dana and Emil return from the Mexico Olympics), there is a letter signed by the couple and by the chess grandmaster Ludek Pachman, in which the trio make their feelings diplomatically but abundantly clear. 'We love our country and we are not abandoning it; we would be unable to live without it. However we are afraid that soon it will be impossible to live in it if our leaders surrender further. We fear a new age of darkness in which insincerity will be a virtue, a lie will be the truth, and silence will be an existential necessity'.

Six months later, the same file records, 'On 14th April 1969 students at Charles University in Prague organised a "Day of Prague Spring politics". There were meetings and discussions with speakers.

'*[the informant]* arrived at 10am to a meeting with approximately 1000 people. Zatopek was being interviewed. *[the informant]* does not know how long Zatopek had been talking before his arrival.

[Questions from the floor, answers from Zatopek]

Q: Did the events in August 1968 lead to armed conflict with the Soviet Army?
A: As far as I am aware, no. However in several units there was some sort of disagreement. For example in Horsovsky Tyn a Czechoslovak commander of a tank unit ordered our tank drivers to leave the barracks through the back before the Soviet soldiers arrived, which our soldiers, with exemplary morals and enthusiasm, obeyed without hesitation. Then when the Soviet tank commander came to negotiate with our guys, our unit commander said to him, "What do you want to negotiate, after all you're surrounded." Our commander was then taken away.

Then Colonel ZATOPEK discussed the fact that, for example:

"For the last 50 years our army has not inflicted any wounds... When, some time ago, I was serving as a warrant officer at the Ministry of National Defence, I received a command to set up an emergency military unit for the Prague garrison. The emergency unit, concentrated in the door to the building of the Central Committee, was not used and the next morning it was disbanded."

Q: What were or are the chances of a coup in Czechoslovakia?
A: I'm as informed on this matter as you are. However I heard that apparently the possibility of it was discussed in connection with the visits of Marshall Grečka, General Bedrich, General Dvorak and Minister Dzuf. They could manage it because they have a lot of power between them. However I think it is unrealistic.

Colonel ZATOPEK further spoke about the fact that...

"... I'm now in charge of athletes at Dukla (army sports club). In accordance with a command from the Ministry of National Defence, some officers were discharged for demonstrating anti-Soviet tendencies. The MMO also said that some commanding officers should notify their seniors of their morally political stance and state whether they support the alliance and cooperation with the Soviet Union or not. If the answer is in the negative, they are threatened with being discharged from the armed forces.

I decided to tell the athletes at Dukla that I did not want any written statements from them and that I have informed the commanding officers that everything here is in order. I did this because I had previously told them that I will give them three options: the first is socialist cooperation and alliance with the Soviet Union, the second is socialism with a human face, the third is for socialism and democracy including extensive contact with the West. Everyone supported this third variant.

… If there was more financial investment into our training, which we all know is severely neglected, than into our army, we would certainly do better. Luxembourg, because it is such a small state, abolished its army, since in today's world it is considered unnecessary for its state. At least in our army young men gain skills like, for example, driving, cooking, radio operating and so on. This is good for general life.

….We must eliminate anger from our thinking as it never leads anywhere good. You of course know that in revolutions anger leads people to beheading – so it was for Robespierre, for Marat, for the Hussites and eventually even the Communists did it. I am a peace-loving man and I am against anger. Thoughts of armed resistance against the Soviets are illogical and unrealistic.

Colonel ZATOPEK's appearance at Charles University, Prague concluded with applause.

Conclusion: Even though, in my opinion, Colonel ZATOPEK tried in many of his responses to calm and placate several "heated" young people, I note that in relation to the current domestic political situation his responses were inappropriate given that he, as a member of the Czechoslovak army, is not well enough informed or politically erudite to be able to publicly talk to such a gathering about serious political problems.   Pavel HLOUCHA'

Regarding comrade Hloucha's conclusion, I observe only that someone who would cite Robespierre and Marat and 14th century religious revolutionaries is hardly lacking in political erudition. But elsewhere in the files, there are similar remarks about Zátopek from much earlier in his life, bemoaning the lack of adequate political instruction at his military academy; and recommending that he be sent for 're-education'. That never happened, as far as I can tell. His services as a superlative athlete were doubtless considered far more valuable to the regime. As for the Luxembourg Army, Zátopek may have been referring to the fact that two years previously, Luxembourg abandoned military service, and began to rely on a volunteer force, which still exists.

51.

The entr'acte between the Soviet-led invasion of late August 1968 and the full implementation of 'normalisation' over six months later was shattered by one of the most historically totemic acts of defiance against totalitarianism – Jan Palach immolating himself in Wenceslas Square on January 16, 1969. He died in hospital three days later. His funeral turned into a major protest against the Occupation. On February 25, another student, Jan Zajíc emulated Palach, also in Wenceslas Square, and two months later in the provincial town of Jihlava, Evžen Plocek did the same. It was only revealed much later that a 59 year old accountant, a former member of the Polish wartime resistance, Ryszard Siwiec had burned himself to death four months prior to Palach, as a protest against the invasion. Although that self-immolation was filmed, the Polish authorities successfully covered it up, and Palach almost certainly did not know of it. The celebrated Polish film director Agnieszka Holland was a student at the Prague Film School (FAMU) throughout this whole period, and in 2013 made an atmospheric television mini-series, entitled *Hořící Keř* (Burning Bush).

The work is a dramatization of events surrounding Palach's suicide, especially the attempt of his mother Libuše Palachová to sue the reactionary politician Vilém Nový over his allegation that Palach had been a dupe for revolutionaries, among them Zátopek. Nový claimed that a group of four prominent signatories of the *2000 Words Manifesto* – the others were chess grandmaster Ludek Pachman, the writers Vladimir Škutina and Pavel Kohout plus a student activist Luboš Holeček - had conspired to convince Palach that the liquid he was to pour over himself though flammable would not burn him. The 'Cold Fire' case was a further sensation in that troubled period, but one in which Zátopek, seemingly would not emerge with any credit.

The quintet accused by Nový bought a civil case against him, which was eventually joined to that of Libuše Palachová. (The film does not feature a Zátopek character). The affair dragged on through to the summer, with Nový refusing to answer the summons, claiming parliamentary immunity. The case would finally be thrown out months later, but Zátopek distinguished himself by going to the final hearing and withdrawing his case before the court. His co-claimants and fans were horrified at this volte-face, and the betrayal was made worse two years later, when Zátopek recanted his signing of the *2000 Words Manifesto*. Asked again about the Nový case, in an interview published on July 20, 1971, Zátopek told the Communist daily *Rudé právo*, 'We pursued the lawsuit as a result of our bruised egos. But I felt that in the end our arguments landed us in the role of the accused. It was clear to me that it was in fact our group which was entirely wrong..... the longer I sat there, the more I became aware of the pettiness of our complaint. So I said outright, look, I don't want to bring a lawsuit just because something offended me. I am not an enemy of socialism. If this goes against socialism, then please forgive me. And so the trial collapsed.'

Despite this confirmation of his about-turn, historian and biographer, Pavel Kosatík thinks he sees Zátopek's rationale. "It was difficult, because all his friends were sitting in the court and he surprised them. The reason was his chief in the army must have told him, we will arrest you for 20 years. Because that was a sentence he repeated many times, I could be arrested for 20 years. Someone had obviously said this to him. I would think it would be impossible to arrest Emil Zátopek for ten or twenty years. I find it hard to believe, but he obviously believed it. Some of the other petitioners, his friends, they were arrested, for a year or two or three, so it was rational for him to imagine that it could happen to him too".

Yet contemporary with this 'betrayal' is the curious case of the *Ten Points Petition*. Because, while his career and social life were slowly unravelling, it seems that Zátopek got involved in another public challenge to the regime and its Soviet puppet-masters. According to Michael Žantovský, in his biography of Vacláv Havel, on the anniversary of the invasion, that's to say, August 21, 1969, Zátopek was one of the signatories of the *Ten Points Petition*, calling for various reforms. However, Zántovský notes that Zátopek's signature is missing from the copy of the *Ten Points* held in the Vacláv Havel Library. Nonetheless, the story again underlines, Zátopek's continuing opposition at this point to the status-quo, and his central involvement with the principal opposition.

52.

An editorial in the Moscow-based *Sovietsky Sport* on January 1, 1969 signalled the beginning of the campaign to strip Zátopek of his titles and privileges. The article contends, 'Zátopek has shown duplicity both in his words, and in nurturing a deep hatred and hostility towards socialism, even though his own access to the highest echelons of sport has been solely thanks to the development of socialism in Czechoslovakia'.

And further, 'the Olympic champion, who has pretended for many years to be a friend of both the Soviet Union and her athletes has lined up alongside the enemies of his country, the enemies of socialism. He benefited from his trip to Mexico (1968 Olympic Games) in making anti-Soviet statements and spreading stupid rumours which glorify bourgeois propaganda'.

In *Le Terrassier de Prague*, French writer Pierre Naudin details some dates of action taken in the ensuing months against Zátopek:

January 19, 1969, Colonel Zátopek is relieved of all his duties as Sports Director at the Ministry of Sport. He was named deputy coach at a Prague athletics club: DUKLA.

April 22, 1969, he is suspended by the army: 'for having circulated false information, and for conduct contrary to Ministry of Defence orders'. An enquiry is opened into his case.

April 28, 1969, a journalist from the Swedish publication Aftonbladet delivers to him a proposal from the Swedish Athletic Association, offering him work as a coach. He turns down the offer, saying he would never be given permission to leave the country.

August 18, 1969, Zátopek loses his stripes, and is told to quit the army post by October 1st.

October 27, 1969, he is expelled from the Communist Party, along with 19 members of the central Committee Praesidium. One hundred and seventy three others are sacked from the Party administration. On the same day, under a headline, 'Glory and Responsibility,' Rudé právo accuses Zátopek of, 'having agitated alongside various anti-socialist and anti-Soviet renegade opportunists, and helping to unleash a social crisis, which threatened the very foundations of society'. Further, he was criticised for having consorted with foreign journalists and despite his status as Colonel, having criticised the army publicly. But even worse, 'he made public a certain number of army documents containing classified information relevant to national security'.

December 8, 1969, Zátopek is officially expelled from the army for, according the Ministry of Defence, 'having divulged information destined solely for army purposes, and for having altered such information so as to conceal the truth'.

June 28, 1970, following Dubček's own expulsion from the Communist Party, Zátopek is relieved of his final official post, on the Steering Committee for Physical Education.

53.

When I first met Dana for the purposes of this book, in May 2014, she began by telling me that she was writing her own book about life with Emil. But, she reassured me, "I'm only telling you that, so you'll know. I'm very happy to talk to you, and answer any of your questions. I was angry with this French writer, there are so many mistakes. This is why I began writing my book, it's only true". This confused me momentarily, because I'd been in the National Library the previous day, reading a little known volume called *Le Terrassier de Prague* by Pierre Naudin, and published over 40 years previous. Then, suddenly I realised that Dana was referring to *Courir*, a post-modern curiosity by Prix Goncourt winner, Jean Echenoz, which had recently been translated into Czech. The hero in *Courir*, published in 2008, is referred to only as Émile, French-style, until over three-quarters of the way through when 'Zátopek' appears. I'd enjoyed the book, but saw little value in attempting to explain to a 91 year old, albeit a bright and coherent one, the process of re-imagining a life in literature. I'd got my own furrow to plough.

'Terrassier' – the word means labourer or navvy - had raised enough questions anyway. I'd been assured by Dana, by TV journalist Škorpíl, and by old friend Kořán that, contrary to popular legend, Emil had never worked as a bin-man (garbage collector) in Prague, and that when he was exiled to the provinces to work, it was on a geological survey team. It may be that this was the cover story from a regime that was already embarrassed at how they were treating a national hero, and everyone else went along with it, because Naudin has some very specific information on this from a variety of people. Naudin had a colourful life himself. A working class boy who, early in life had many manual labouring jobs, he graduated to being a successful writer, author of dozens of popular medieval romances. He was also a keen cyclist and long distance runner, and had gone to a European Masters' or Veterans' road running championship in Karlovy Vary (Karlsbad) in the early 1970s. Since Zátopek was working close-by in the Ore Mountains, he hoped to see him at the championship or pay him a visit, since his post-normalisation plight was still

making headlines around Europe. But he was warned off trying to find Zátopek by a variety of people, who said that any meetings with westerners would only exacerbate Emil's problems. However, he was reassured that Zátopek was not working on a geological survey team, but was no more than a labourer. The latter was certainly the case when he worked at the mines in Jáchymov, as you will read later when I quote Petr Loukota, who had known him there.

According to Naudin, 'The first person to give me information on Zátopek was a French national, who said she knew him well. Here's what she told me:

I was in Prague when they made him a bin-man after kicking him out of the army. But that didn't last long, because when folks recognised him behind the truck, they came to their windows and applauded him... his workmates refused to let him collect the bins from the pavements, so he either walked or ran behind the cart.... The following day, in the neighbourhood where he was due to collect the rubbish, it was the young folks mostly came down into the street, some to applaud, and other to empty the bins themselves into the cart. That's why he was quickly sent to work way outside Prague – a sort of exile.'

She and two others, one a running friend of Emil, the other an organiser of the championships, all told Naudin that he was not working on a geological team, but was simply digging holes for telegraph poles. For obvious reasons, Naudin does not name the informants, but he quotes the running friend, who clearly sees what must ultimately happen to Emil.

'He can't resist forever... he needs to resign himself... he'll have to say that he made a mistake, that he regrets his actions... that's what they're waiting for.... he won't be the first.. they'll make him back the new regime, and then they'll leave him in peace... folks won't blame him, they haven't forgotten who he was, or what he did... they're not fools.'

Incidentally, political historian Pavel Kosatík, who published his own book on Zátopek, entitled, *Emil-Běžec* (Emil-Runner) in late 2015 told me that he had searched high and low for a photo of Emil when he was working as a labourer in the Ore Mountains. "I wasn't able to find any snap, any photograph that people made with him. You would think someone would say, I should make a photo with him, but they didn't. Maybe there was a fear, I don't know. People there still remember him, as a sad and comical looking figure, in sports' dress (track suit?) and a beret, working hard, of course, and twice a day running for beer for his two friends working with him. He said he had to run as quickly as possible so the beer wouldn't go flat. I found a place where he worked in a mine in the 70s, and there's a stone in the deep forest, and it says, 'Here Emil Zátopek made water'. It's still there".

54.

The circumstances of Zátopek's recantation of his support for Dubček and the signing of the *2000 Words Manifesto* seem serendipitous, and indeed Dana told me that when she found out the first thing she asked is why he did it. She was rather more forceful in an interview with *Lidovky* magazine in 2012, saying, 'I really gave him what for'. Because, as with his gift of an Olympic gold medal to Ron Clarke, he had not told Dana in advance, presumably to avoid her opposition. When we talked about this, it was the only time during our several interviews that Dana did not look at me when she responded. "He was asked many times to write an apology, and finally he agreed. I didn't know about this, and when I asked why he did this, he said, 'Sorry, you are right, but when you are near a very deep hole, you can go right to the edge, but you can't jump in'. This was his answer, (and here she switched to English) 'Life is very beautiful, and I am no hero'."

He said the same thing - 'I am no hero' - to his old friend Lada Kořán, in response to a similar question. But, having been treated as such by so many for so long, with only the preceding blip of withdrawal of his case against Vilém Nový two years earlier, meant that his reputation with many, though not all Czechoslovaks was going to be forever tainted. I earlier mentioned Věra Čáslavská's only public stance prior to signing the *2000 Words Manifesto* as being a brief piece in a student magazine defending Zátopek against a satirical poem it had published, criticising him. My principal translator Esther Jones-Russell came up with what seems to me an excellent interpretation of said poem.

It was only last year he supported
an ethic to which he would stick
but he'd soon go back to Novotný
if it meant he were part of the clique.

Novotný was the pre-liberalisation President and First Secretary, deposed in favour of Svoboda and Dubček, and the poem was published before the

Soviet-led invasion, following which Zátopek proved himself as a pillar of the opposition and a man of the people *par excellence*. Yet the student-poet, presumably criticising Colonel Zátopek on the basis of his being a member of the establishment proved to be remarkably prescient on the business of turning coats.

Brian Freemantle is a successful writer, principally of spy novels, but as a journalist until the mid-1970s, he was foreign editor of the British newspaper, the *Daily Mail*. Freemantle had gone to Prague in spring of 1971 with an introduction and phone number for Zátopek, from Free Czech contacts in London. When we spoke in early 2016, he complained inevitably that memories of a trip to Prague over four decades ago were relatively thin, but he remembered the basics, and much of it fitted in with what he referred to as, 'cloak and dagger,' ie his stock in trade as a spy novelist. "I'd gone to get a feel of what it was like in Czechoslovakia at that time and in those circumstances, and obviously Emil Zátopek being the most famous person at that time, who people in the west could recognise or associate with, it was my idea to try and wrap the story around him… I called the number. I must have tried for two days, at all times of day and night, no reply, no reply, no reply. Then I got a reply, not from Emil Zátopek, and explained who I was, and a meeting was arranged at the Alcron hotel (now the Radisson), I went there, and sat at the bar, and no one came.

"I just sat there, obviously a westerner. No one approached me, I called the number again, and was told that the meeting…. I then realised I wasn't actually going to meet Emil Zátopek, but somebody else. I said could I meet him, and was told it was impossible to meet him, they said no. He was a very nervous man at the time, with every good reason; I mean, he was virtually under house arrest…. After about four days, I actually spoke to him, I think again it was about four phone calls, I had to give a list of the questions I wanted to ask, obviously I wanted him to be as forthright as possible, and that was the last thing at the time he wanted to be, and we finally agreed a connection and when we finally agreed the questions, it was a telephone interview which lasted I think about, oh, I don't know, about ten minutes. There was background noise, he was not by himself, he was with friends…

"He sounded very apprehensive, to the point of being frightened. When we were actually talking, I got the impression - he never came back straightaway in the way that I'm coming back to you, immediately - I always got the impression that the question was being considered by other people with him in the room, whether it was safe or not safe. I think there were people looking after him, or wanting to look after him, and wanting him not to make any mistakes. I wasn't setting out to make him make a mistake, but they were very cautious, and I think that their caution built upon his caution. It was a very difficult time to be in Prague, there were a lot of Russians about. I didn't think that I was under any particular observation, but everyone was very nervous. No one really knew where it was going to end, and where they were going to be. I didn't feel under any pressure there, then again, I had a passport to leave. So I had an interview, but that was the circumstances. At the time, I considered I'd done quite well, because he wouldn't speak to people. Once I'd convinced myself that I was speaking to him, they asked who'd given me the number, and I had to use a Christian name, so that was my credibility, as it were. The Czech people in London I was dealing with at the time were very pleased with it, and so was I. I regret the fact that I never got him face to face, but I did get him to the extent that you see in the interview".

In the article published on May 3, 1971 under the headline, ZATOPEK… THE WILL TO WIN IS CRUSHED, Freemantle wrote, 'The Communist regime in Czechoslovakia has broken the spirit of the country's most famous sportsman, Emil Zatopek. The 48 year old deposed army colonel, who won three gold medals for his country in the 1952 Helsinki Olympics, told me, 'I am reconciled to conditions in my country. Once I was unhappy, but not now. There seems little point'. There was a pause while he sought for the correct expression. Then he said: 'I exist'.' The article goes on to quote Zátopek on his brief tenure as a garbage collector in Prague – 'But people would gather round and some even helped me,' before describing being seconded to a team travelling the country, 'making test bores for construction work'. The article ends with Zátopek saying, 'I am reasonably happy. I think Husak (Gustav, the new party leader) is a good man. He is very intelligent. He has said Zatopek is a sportsman who should only talk about sport and not involve himself in politics and perhaps he is right'.'

It was three months before there was any response; but on July 20, 1971, the Communist party newspaper, *Rudé právo* (Red Truth) published a lengthy rebuttal of the *Mail's* claims, based on an interview with Zátopek at their offices the previous week. After denying that he ever worked as a bin-man, saying it was a rumour first published in the West German newspaper, *Die Welt*, and claiming that he now worked on a geological survey team, the questions turn to the true reason for the interview. The seminal quotes, which travelled the world are, 'I don't want to make any excuses, but trust me that even before signing the 2000 Words I had my doubt about this declaration.... It was twice as bad for me because I had just returned with a delegation from the Soviet Union where I often sensed and heard fears that we were opening our arms to the anti-socialist world and that supporting these tendencies could lead to the destruction of the regime..... when they brought it to me to sign I said, please don't be foolish, but one person who was with us said, look, Mr Zátopek, at all the famous people who have signed it.... I said that to sign my name and be among such significant people was certainly something, but it was still an imprudent affair. But no, you're right. I signed it.

'Then I heard the Party Chairman's statement which condemned the *2000 Words* as a politically irresponsible document. Let me tell you that really played on my conscience. I am truly sorry that I was among those wild people who in fact fanned the flames which could have erupted into wildfire and could have really jeopardised the socialist world.... I was never under any illusions that I had done a praiseworthy thing. Now with hindsight I am able to see that if trends from the *2000 Words* had progressed, it would have been catastrophic: socialism and the socialist regime would have collapsed.'

This whole document has all the hallmarks of having been constructed by the Central Committee; but there is no doubt that Zátopek put his name to it. And I was reminded of my conversation with his oldest training partner, Jindra Roudný when he had told me of the numerous times that Emil had shown him documents and speeches written for him, and complaining to Roudný, 'And they want me to say this!' That presumably was the price for his freedom to travel and otherwise enjoy his celebrity.

In *Le Terrassier de Prague*, published later in 1971, Naudin comments about Zátopek's dismissal of the *Mail's* story. 'To deny that he'd even been a bin-man, when a whole suburb of Prague had witnessed him doing that, is already extraordinary, then to describe digging holes for telegraph poles as 'geological surveying' is even more incredible. But are there not situations, when escape is impossible, and we are not only obliged to give in, but to say or do anything in order to get a bit of peace?' This is a question I put to his old friend, Jindra Roudný, asking, wouldn't you have done the same? Ever the hardliner, Roudný simply said, 'No'.

The *Daily Mail* itself responded immediately. The day following the *Rudé právo* rebuttal, under the headline, 'Zatopek forced to toe the party line,' Freemantle begins, 'Czechoslovakia's most famous sportsman Emil Zatopek was forced yesterday to support the regime of Gustav Husak.' Freemantle glosses his original piece, and then gives the substance of Zátopek's retraction in *Rudé právo*, before commenting, 'There is no doubt that the interview in Rude Pravo, from a man still regarded as a hero in his country, stems from government pressure to make the present regime acceptable.... The man who once threatened to fight Russian tanks with his bare hands and vowed: 'I will never be silenced' was a crushed, subdued man... So abject was Zatopek's apology that it clashed with facts that even the Communists have published. He said he was still a reserve officer in the army and received a pension – contradicting a statement by the Defence Ministry that he had been expelled from the army 'because he violated legal norms'.'

There had however been a precedent for the public recantation, also published in *Rudé právo* over 20 years earlier. It was after the death sentence was passed on Milada Horáková. This time it was a letter, signed Captain Emil Zátopek, referring to, 'The sentence passed...'

The words spoken by Mr. President at the Czechoslovak Union of Youth when citing the old revolutionary song 'let the cruel old world die' are in fact ideas that lead us forward. Yet there are monsters that have wanted to destroy our development and path to socialism.

'All spies and traitors have acted shamefully and foolishly; our nation will never surrender the better living conditions it has fought for, nor will historical progress ever again return to the old days. People are convinced of the fortune of socialism, its harmony and cooperation and they will never have their rights ripped from their grasp.

'Saboteurs condemn themselves with their own divisive actions and by

preparing for war against their own nation.

'The verdict is a warning for anybody in the Czechoslovak republic looking to achieve reprehensible goals. All of us are working together to build a better life and anyone who wants to disrupt our collective work will end up where the band of spies and saboteurs have ended up.

'The sentence was passed by the entire Czechoslovak nation.

'As a member of the Czechoslovak army I can see that the verdict is a command that comes from the honest work of all of our labourers in order for our soldiers to preserve a peaceful life.'

As well as in *Rudé právo* itself, I found the above letter reproduced in a document entitled, 'The propaganda campaign accompanying the trial of Milada Horáková and co,' edited by Pavlína Formánová and Petr Koura, which is in the files of the *Institute for Contemporary History*. The editors of the document refer to the writer Ota Filip unearthing this denunciation years later, and criticizing Zátopek's mean-mindedness. 'In this article,' writes Filip, of Zátopek's letter to *Rudé právo*, 'he welcomes the death penalty against Horáková, an alleged agent of Western imperialists, as a victory for socialism.'

But Filip himself was later unmasked as a secret police (StB) informant and collaborator, and Formánová and Koura comment, 'in our opinion, in the context of the entire campaign it is unequivocally impossible to evaluate Zátopek's text in such a way. This text does condemn 'spies' and 'traitors' but only in general terms. Zátopek does not name a single person (which was not common in other texts of that ilk); he does not personally offend anybody and it is evident that although he signed his name under these few lines, he does not identify with them too much. This is no surprise: although Zátopek was an icon of Czechoslovak sport, he was married to the niece of General Sergej Ingr, former minister for the Czech government-in-exile in London who, since the war, had campaigned against Communist rule from abroad.'

I asked Dana about General Ingr, and she corrected one minor point. He was not her uncle, she said, he was her godfather, a friend of her father's. The pair had been in the army together, and at one point had fought alongside the Russians, before Dana's dad was captured and sent to Dachau. "It's a big tradition in Moravia, to have a godfather, someone to look out for you, apart from your parents".

55.

As our visit to the Svarnost mine in Jáchymov was concluding, I asked if there was anyone who still remembered Zátopek from the 1970s. There certainly was, replied the foreman; and he still worked part-time as an electrician. He was on holiday that week, but the foreman was sure he was still in town. A phone call confirmed that, and we set up an appointment for the following morning. Both Dana and Štěpán Škorpíl (who admitted he didn't get to know the Zátopeks until after Emil returned from exile) stated categorically that Emil never worked underground at Jáchymov. Emil may have said that in order not to worry Dana further, and it had become generally accepted. Because our interviewee was adamant that, though he could not remember the exact year, "sometime in the early 1970s, it wasn't long, maybe two months, but he was labouring on the 12th floor at Svarnost".

Petr Loukota was a short, stout, vibrant man on the threshold of his 68th birthday, three days later. He came early the next morning after our trip down the mine, to meet us at the Radium Palace. He was on his way into the mountains, to visit his 93 year old father, who still lived alone, but needed a hand with manual tasks, like gardening from time to time. I'd been surprised to see that the mine galleries that we visited the previous day were close to two metres (over six feet) high, but Loukota confirmed that he, at around 1.65m was the perfect height for the former workings. "If you were one metre seventy or more, you had to walk like this." he said, leaning his head onto his shoulder. He couldn't remember the exact year that Zátopek had worked at Svarnost, but thought it had to be around 1973, "because I was about 27," which tallies with the years of Zátopek's exile from Prague to work as a labourer.

"It was extraordinary to see someone like Emil Zátopek working at the mine alongside us. It was a big event in our lives to meet someone like him. When he came there, he was greeted like the celebrity that he was. We were overwhelmed. We only met during working hours, on the 12th floor. There were no other political prisoners in Svarnost mine. The uranium was exhausted by this time, and from 1964, the mine where Mr Zátopek worked, was handed over to the Jáchymov spa. A cross-cut (corridor) between the mines had been constructed in the 1950s, and the uranium part was blocked off, and the pits were flooded, and Svarnost was isolated. Where Mr Zátopek worked was actually 360 metres below the flooded pits.

"Emil was working all day at the new digging, at Behonek Spring. He was pushing wagons filled with pipes, conduits, ducts and sacks of cement and stones or gravel. They were very heavy, but he seemed very happy to do this work, he said it kept him fit (He would have been over 50 at this time). Because he wanted to keep himself in condition, he loaded it all himself and made sure it was full. He wasn't very tall, and he wasn't overweight, but he was very wiry, very sinewy. In the mineshaft, it was an advantage to be smaller, because he didn't have to bend. If he hadn't been in good physical condition, he wouldn't have been able to do this work, push these heavy wagons. We talked about his sports career with him, but also about politics, everything under the sun. I remember him as very cheerful person. He seemed to be a well-balanced person. I think it was like Mrs Čáslavská, he took it as something he had to do for his beliefs. He had a very positive view of life, very cheerful. He seemed satisfied with his lot".

56.

Even though he recanted in the middle of 1971, it was still four years before the regime allowed Zátopek to work back in Prague. And that concession was undoubtedly helped by pressure, inadvertent in some cases, from foreign sources. It began in 1972, when he was invited, as was Věra Čáslavská, as guest of honour to the Olympic Games in Munich. Zátopek was still labouring in the Ore Mountains in northern Bohemia, and initially his gang boss refused to let him go, saying that with so few people in their group – three on some jobs – he could not afford to lose one member for two weeks. As I quoted his old friend Lada Kořán elsewhere, Zátopek was always well-informed about what was going on behind the scenes, and it seems to have still been the case when he could get back to Prague to see Dana every two weeks or so. In 1998, he told me, "I answered to our authorities I could not go (to Munich). But 27 years after the World War, we had no diplomatic relations with Germany, and before, we probably had 50% of our trade with Germany. We want to invite (Chancellor) Willi Brandt, they said, so Zátopek must go.

"Then in 1973, Paavo Nurmi died – the most famous distance runner in history. The organisers in Finland invited me to the Paavo Nurmi Memorial. Then in 1975, UNESCO wasn't really a sporting organisation, but the president of the (International) Committee for Fair Play in Paris was (Jean) Borotra, and he tried to turn UNESCO towards sport. Every year they award a Fair Play prize, and I won it in 1975. Returning home, I was invited to meet the chief of our Sports Committee - a nice man. He said, what can we do about you? If we get an invitation for you to go abroad, we cannot refuse? You will return to the Sports Committee, and you will be free for invitations. I worked in the information centre here in Prague until I retired (1982)".

Dana was not permitted to travel out of the country with him until 1978, and even that, she told me was a surprise that it came so soon. And in respect of the UNESCO Fair Play award, she said that news of it at home merited all of two lines in *Rudé právo*. That was a lot compared to the attitude to others, as Czech Radio correspondent in London, Jiří Hošek told me. "Zátopek was an icon. The Communists could not dispute or deny his achievements, but because of his stance and his attitudes to the events of 1968/69, he was partially on the blacklist. But the Communists did not go that far away from him as they did, for example in the case of Martina Navrátilová, the famous Czechoslovak tennis player who defected in 1975. She ceased to exist. It was ridiculous, she was completely erased. And even when she was winning one Grand Slam after another, she was just completely ignored.

"The only mention was basically one line - US Open, Flushing Meadow, Finals, Navrátilová, United States defeated Evert-Lloyd, United States, 6-2, 6-2. And that was it. Something very similar happened to Ivan Lendl, even in late 1980s, when from outside you had the impression that the system is already just crumbling. Once he got less and less popular with the Communist leaders, and he was staying outside more and more, and basically his only contact with Czechoslovakia was that he played once or twice a year in the Davis Cup. Also he just disappeared from media coverage. In that respect, it was something similar what happened to Zátopek".

When Zátopek was permitted to accept the invitation to the Olympic Games in Munich, he'd already realised the value of caution. *Runners' World* correspondent Joe Henderson bumped into him at Munich airport after the 1972 Games. Henderson later wrote, 'To me, Zátopek is the finest runner of the past 50 years. I view him that way for how he once raced, but even more so, for how he has continued to live and give. I'd never expected to meet this great man from a then-remote land. But we came together by chance while waiting to board flights out of Munich, Germany, following the 1972 Olympics. After he blew kisses to friends outside the boarding area, I worked up the courage to approach him. "Uh, excuse me, are you Emil Zátopek?" I asked, already knowing he was, but not knowing if he understood English. "Why yes, Zátopek," he answered without missing a beat. "And what is your name, please?" Mine meant nothing to him, but he still took time to talk to me for 20 minutes. Zatopek had come to Munich as a guest of the International Olympic Committee to celebrate the 20th anniversary of his triple victories. "It is odd," he said, "to have all this how do you say it, acclaim? In my country I am just a common man, a nobody". Zátopek didn't talk politics directly, but he was officially a 'nobody' in Czechoslovakia.

When a revolt against the Soviet domination of his country broke out in 1968, he took the wrong side in the struggle and lost his rank as an army colonel. This national hero was reduced to working as a garbage collector and a street sweeper, jobs normally reserved in his country for the mentally retarded. In Munich, Zátopek excused himself and walked toward the plane that would take him to Prague, back to his simple life as a nobody, a man whose name will forever live in Olympic history'.

Zátopek will have been amply reminded of that view of himself while being fêted in Munich, but when he got back to Prague, he gave Dana a far simpler but more telling view of his two weeks away from the road gang. "He told me," Dana said, "for a few days, I was treated as a human being. Then he went back to the same work". Almost a decade after the Soviet invasion there was another attempt at liberalisation, by the *Charter 77* group. Although it was couched in terms such that it would not break any laws, among those of its first signatories to be arrested was the future President, Václav Havel. However, Zátopek, ensconced in the archives of the Sports Ministry had learned his lesson, and didn't go anywhere near. But his internal exile was being relaxed bit by bit, thanks to a man who was ostensibly part of the establishment. When I was beginning my research, Prague Marathon chief Carlo Capalbo urged me to talk to Štěpán Škorpil who was an indefatigable promoter of the Zátopek legend.

I've already told you about Škorpil's introduction to Zátopek via radio transmissions from Helsinki, and later he would become a family friend, ferrying Emil and Dana (and Věra Čáslavská) to schools and sports clubs to give talks during the dark days. As a young decathlete, Škorpil had joined the Dukla athletics club (where Emil was a member) in autumn 1968, but given the momentous events that had just taken place, Zátopek was already out of the door. But Zátopek's return to Prague to work in the Sports Ministry archives was virtually concurrent with the ultimate realisation of Škorpil's broadcasting ambition – becoming sports editor of Czech TV. "I always remember the date, 4/5/75, I started officially," he told me. "In this moment, when there was place for some speech (comment) about athletics, every time, I am going for Emil. And because it was five, six years after this complicated situation, with the (Soviet) Occupation, I started doing short, fifteen, twenty seconds interview with him. But after three years, they had new discussion programmes, and at this moment, it was Emil Zátopek, three, four minutes, looking at world of athletics. And every year after that, it was better and better".

The decade between his retirement and the Velvet Revolution, which would bring him back to a certain prominence consisted of life at home tinkering in Troja, punctuated by visits to give talks to schools and sports clubs – often ferried by Škorpil – with trips abroad, either to receive awards, or be fêted as guest of honour at Olympic Games, World or European Championships. He continued to make friends and devotees wherever he went. US track writer Marc Bloom, editor of the much-missed *The Runner*, the best athletics magazine ever, recalled for me a visit that Zátopek made to New York. "I was privileged to first meet Zátopek in '79 when we were in the early years of *The Runner* and George H (Hirsch, the publisher) engineered bringing Zátopek to NY as a guest of the Marathon. I picked him up at the airport with a writer I'd assigned to do a piece on him. From that moment on, for his entire stay, the man was absolutely enchanting. When he came up to our offices, he would break into song, serenading anyone, treating secretaries with the same respect and indeed love as any exec. Everyone kept saying, "This is the guy who won the Olympic distance triple?" I don't think I'd ever met anyone so humble and gracious".

When I met Zátopek in 1998, he was already a little unsteady on his feet and forgetful, and switching mid-sentence between English and French. And when we met again in 1999, he was even frailer, relying on Dana to support and guide him. As she later told me, he had already had Alzheimer's for several years at that point, although it wasn't obvious, he just seemed old and tired. His final interview with Škorpil dates from around that time. "Our last interview was 40 minutes," Škorpil said. "It was in April '99 (18 months before Zátopek's death), and it is in the archives of the Czech Olympic Committee. It was very difficult, because after every five, six minutes, we had to stop, and Dana would bring some water. And at one moment, his false teeth broke, and Dana had to bring some glue. It was absolutely crazy. And that was the last interview".

57.

In agreeing with Ron Clarke that Emil Zátopek is, if not the greatest long distance runner in history, then the greatest influence on long distance running in history, I intend no disservice to the memory of Paavo Nurmi. The Flying Finn's record, including an almost inconceivable Olympic medal collection of nine golds and two silvers in the middle and long distances is without equal. But by common consent, Nurmi was an hermetic character whose exploits began and ended on the athletics track. Zátopek proved himself both in the stadium and on the streets of Prague, when the occasion demanded. Of course, it is not given to everyone to live in a time and place where 'events' ask more of us. But in 1968, Zátopek was more than equal to that challenge as well.

As a former middle and sometime long distance runner myself, I am perhaps biased, but having been present at some enthralling sprint duels - none more so than Ben Johnson's 'victory'over Carl Lewis at the Olympic Games in Seoul 1988 - I do not quite share the opinion of the lesser known of the Birchfield Harriers' Stewart brothers, Peter, when he greeted the arrival of the sprinters at a UK indoor meeting some four decades ago with, "Here come the fucking circus performers". Lewis too won nine Olympic golds, and I was witness to enough of his victories in adversity to admire his competitive spirit. Unfortunately I was also privy to a number of tantrums which would have shamed a pre-teen. In any case, it is ridiculous to include relay medals in any individual's tally (just as it is to count team race medals, which are included in Nurmi's haul). Also natural talent has far more sway in sprinting, and the work-load is trivial compared to that of even an 800 metres runner, let alone a marathoner. Lewis's four consecutive Olympic long-jump golds are far more meritorious in my view than his sprint victories. So much can go wrong in a technical event like the long-jump.

Maybe it's my distaste for the person that colours my view. Al Oerter's four successive Olympic golds in the discus are more valuable in my opinion, since on none of those occasions was Oerter the favourite. Indeed, in Rome 1960, he was throwing with a heavily bandaged shoulder. That is triumph in adversity writ large. I only met Oerter once, in his dotage, ie well over 40. He was still throwing world class distances, but it was the fact that he was cavorting, if a giant can cavort, at a reception with a blonde nymph - another good reason for favouring Big Al.

It is highly unlikely, if not impossible that anyone should emulate Zátopek and win all three distance golds at the Olympic Games. Even with the benefit of blood doping - and having questioned him on the subject, I have no doubts – Lasse Virén* could only finish fifth in the Olympic marathon in Montreal 1976, in the wake of his second successive 5000/10,000 metres double. For the record, prior to Zátopek that double had only been accomplished once before, by Hannes Kohlemainen of Finland in 1912. Since then it has been achieved six more times, making eight out of the 23 times (up to London 2012) that the two track distance events have been contested in the history of the modern Olympic Games. What militates against a repeat of the Olympic triple nowadays is the wholesale professionalism (for want of a better term) of marathoning. The big city marathon boom which began in earnest in the 1980s, with increasingly enormous prize and appearance money (not to mention contestants) has led to the creation of a coterie of specialists, who never race on the track, and against whom Olympic track competitors – having already had three hard races inside four or five days, ie 10,000 metres final, then heat and final of the 5000 metres – have little chance.

In Zátopek's day, marathoners tended to be those who couldn't cut it on the track, or who had graduated to the marathon late in their careers. Zátopek's 'shadow' Mimoun is a case in point, as is Mihalić, the Yugoslav who finished second to Mimoun in Melbourne 1956. Mimoun was a very successful track runner (five silver medals, remember, behind Zátopek), and only turned to the marathon at age 36 – and won. Four years later in Rome, Abebe Bikila who, as far as I can tell never ran either 5000 or 10,000 metres outside Ethiopia, introduced a whole new era. This is not to imply that Zátopek was running against dilettantes. He won the triple in the prime of his running life, and he was competing against the best in the world. His winning time may have been over two minutes slower than the then world record of Jim Peters, but times are insignificant in championships races. And in any case, Peters dropped out of the race, crushed I would venture by Zátopek's insouciance.

After his retirement, Nurmi went into construction, but also opened a haberdashery in Helsinki. In August 1950, on a visit to the Finnish capital for a 5000 metres race, Zátopek went to the shop with the intention of seeking Nurmi's signature for a 'peace accord,' a sporting version of the NATO-Soviet agreement signed in Stockholm earlier in the year. Alerted to Zátopek's visit, Nurmi went AWOL. Forty years later, Zátopek told US sportswriter Mike Sandrock, quoted in his book, *Running with the Legends*, 'Nurmi was famous, but I never spoke with him. It's no wonder.... He was chief of a construction company. It was a capitalist system, and I was a representative of another system... Sportsmen were sometimes used for propaganda, so it was no wonder he would not be able to sign'.

Nurmi was briefly married, and had a son, who eventually ran close to his father's best time at 1500 metres, without making any substantial mark elsewhere in athletics. But let's give the last word on Nurmi to his inheritor, a man who could have not have been more different in character and personality. In an interview with Rich Benyo, the editor of *Marathon & Beyond*, in California in the early 1990s, Zátopek said, 'Paavo Nurmi, he was best long distance runner; he won most gold medals in the Olympic Games. He was a runner, he was a coach, he was his psychologist, his masseur, everything. But he had only one life. He got married, and after one year, his lady returned home to mother and said, he is married to his training and not to me'.

* Before the libel lawyers start sharpening their blue pencils, let me point out that blood doping was not against the rules of the game when Virén won his gold medals, hence his stock response when asked about blood-doping, "I did nothing illegal".

Virén's contemporary, Kaarlo Maaninka, who won silver and bronze medals in Moscow 1980, did admit to blood-doping but, again, the procedure was still not banned at that time. However, another Finn, Martti Vainio was busted when the blood he had withdrawn, then re-injected later – to give him a turbo-boost – proved to be laced with the steroids he'd also been taking. A dope-test was never better named.

58.

The taxi driver who took me from Zlín station to Želechovice didn't speak much English, but recognised Roudný as soon as he saw him, and a brief conversation established the motive for my trip. When the cabbie picked me up again to go back to the station, he asked if I knew that a statue of Zátopek had recently been unveiled at the athletics stadium in Zlín. Since I had a couple of hours to spare until my train back to Prague, and was intending only to have a stroll around the city centre campus of Tomaš Bat'a University – the only evidence nowadays of the vast enterprise which had been run down by the Communists – I got the driver to drop me off at the track which was only a few minutes' walk from the centre.

Now, there are three statues of Zátopek that I know of, and while two are in eminently sensible locations, they are all in strange settings. The odd one out, covered in pigeon shit, stands among shrubs beside Sazka House, the HQ of the national lottery building on an otherwise empty suburban road into Prague. It is a copy of the bronze at the Olympic Museum in Lausanne (sculpted by Jaroslav Broz) which stands in the garden near the back entrance, facing the museum itself. But as Štěpán Škorpil points out (he attended the unveiling, in 2002), "In Lausanne, he is running towards the museum; and everybody at the opening ceremony said he should be by the lake, because Emil gave a sense of freedom, and this position is restricted".

Similarly, the sculpture by Radim Hanke at the stadium in Zlín – formerly the Stadium of Youth, where Emil first saw Dana in early 1948 - is not on a forecourt or in front of the small stand, but at the 200 metres mark, ie the opposite side of the track to the finish line; and, in this case is crammed in a smallish space between the track and a chain-link fence beside a road, across from which is a school. They are all, in their way, cramped, some sort of marmoreal reflection on the ultimate fate of the most exuberant long distance runner in history?

***

As for Roudný, it was he who first alerted me to the fact that there might be more skeletons in Zátopek's back cupboard than the recantation of his support for the Prague Spring movement. When I was preparing to go back to Prague for another round of research, in spring 2015, I emailed Roudný, and asked if I might come to see him again. "I don't know what more I can tell you," he replied. But we agreed that I would call him when I arrived in Prague. What I particularly wanted to follow up was one of his final quotes to me, just before I left Želechovice. "There are things that I will never tell about Emil; and about Dana too. I will take them to the grave". He was as good as his word. I opened my email on a sunny Wednesday morning in London, May 13, 2015, to discover that Roudný had died four days earlier.

59.

It is clear that Emil Zátopek had always been an open-hearted character who would do anything for anyone if he could. His complementary frankness (or as Žantovský would have it, his big mouth) could and did get him into trouble, frequently. But he was no one's fool. He could be diplomatic, even evasive when necessary. Witness his statement, the one he was forced to make as a soldier and member of the nomenklatura, on Milada Horáková, prior to her execution in 1950. As the report for the *Institute for Contemporary History* emphasises, unlike other such statements at the time, he indicted no one personally, speaking/writing in the most general terms. But, elsewhere, his ingenuousness shone through.

You will recall his old friend Kořán's testimony about Zátopek embracing him warmly right in front of the secret police, when they met for the first time in a decade. Contrast that behaviour with Roudný saying that people built second houses out in the countryside specifically so that they could spend weekends talking freely with their friends, knowing that in the bars, shops, workplaces, anywhere public, everyone had to be careful what they were saying. Historian Pavel Kosatík recalled a telling event. "When he stopped running, he made a short interview, which surprised me, because he expressed his private feelings about running. He said he had to run, but he used the term, 'I was crazy,' that it was an obsession; that he had to do it. I was surprised because this was not a time when people talked about themselves frankly. And *he* did. It was maybe even dangerous to say, 'I was crazy, I didn't know what I was doing, and so on'. He was a soldier, a man in a prominent position. He was able to reflect on his situation personally, and it was very nice".

All of this was leading up to the events of 1968 when, it could almost be predicted, Colonel Zátopek would open his big mouth once too often. It may be that, having got away without being censured for his views for so long, he thought he could continue. But, as Kosatík succinctly observed, "In 1952, he knew his worth, in 1968, he did not". In other words, when he faced down the regime over Jungwirth's participation in the Helsinki Olympics, he held all the aces. By the time of the Soviet invasion, he was little more than the joker in the pack. And as such was disposable.

Yet even after his exile, he didn't change. When TV journalist Škorpil was trying to reintroduce Zátopek to the public after his exile, his boss was right to say it could only be taped interviews at first. Because at the very first debate, Emil insisted on telling it like it was. Škorpil recalled, "It was a difficult time for Czech people to travel. They could go to the eastern countries, Bulgaria, Romania, the Black Sea, for example, but not to the West. At this time, Emil and Dana had been all around the world - Indonesia, India, Mexico, USA. So at this (TV) discussion, first half was my job, my questions for Emil and Dana, and second half of the evening was questions from the audience. And every time, I say to the people, you can ask absolutely all, nothing is closed, nothing is sacred. And they asked, for example, in Germany, in France, in Great Britain, how are the people? And Emil says they are free to do what they want. And the next day, our redaction (editors) say, is he a crazy man?"

It may be that, approaching 60 years of age, Zátopek finally realised that nothing worse was going to happen to him, and just didn't care. Or, more likely, this was how he was, and always had been, and he wasn't going to change now. Zátopek wasn't the only person to come up short when pitched against the Soviet juggernaut and its acolytes in Prague. Many people (like Kořán) would argue that he had little choice other than to recant. But his biggest problem in terms of national perception is that there was someone else almost as famous and as high-achieving as himself who also said no but, in contrast continued to say no.

Czech Radio correspondent in London, Jiří Hošek gives the contemporary view. "(Věra) Čáslavská is perceived as a much more important personality, especially because of her engagement in the events of '89, because of her friendship with Václav Havel. What she did, and the way she protested (at the Mexico Olympics) against the Soviet invasion in 1968 was much stronger than the one of Zátopek. So people who study the CVs of Čáslavská and Zátopek, and who know what Zátopek did after the trial of Horáková, and who know even after 1968, after normalisation, this process of very dark Communism after 1969, they see that the moral credit of Čáslavská is a lot higher than that of Zátopek. Secondly, Čáslavská was already famous when people were watching TV, so they saw her perform in Tokyo, and especially in Mexico, at this extremely sensitive time. And Zátopek basically could only be seen in black and white amateur footage, and vintage photography. So those 15 years between the triumphs of Zátopek and Čáslavská ... and Zátopek's health was already deteriorating in 1990s.... he did not have a chance to stand up after the fall of Communism and make some strong statement. I'm taking nothing away from him, we all make mistakes, and I think he must have deeply regretted this, there must have been this massive pressure and propaganda – 'they are the post-Nazi foes, enemies of Czechoslovakia,' - everyone was saying it. But it seems in Zátopek's case, he was always trying to protect himself, trying to find some back door".

60.

Bob Phillips is a (running) generation older than me, and one of life's gentlemen. He was a *BBC Radio* athletics commentator for years, and has been editing the highly regarded *Track Stats* magazine, it seems, for decades. Among his many books is the excellent *Zá-to-pek! Zá-to-pek! Zá-to-pek!* published in 2002. But when he heard that I was researching his hero, he contacted me immediately to wish me well, and he supplied a brief (as he put it) 'stream of consciousness' comment, which crystallises the impact that Zátopek had on an unsuspecting western world during the colourless post-war period.

'The late 1940s and the 1950s was the time of the Cold War and we were constantly being told by our political leaders that everyone east of the Iron Curtain was our enemy. But then Emil came to the 1948 Olympics at Wembley and won the 10,000 and spectacularly lost the 5000 through mis-judging Gaston Reiff's lead, and he seemed equally happy with both races. There's also the famous story that he went to show his gold medal to Dana at the college where she was staying with the Czech women's team and managed to drop it in the swimming pool and then had to strip off and dive in to retrieve it.

'This wasn't the behaviour we'd been told to expect from a Communist athlete – they were supposed to be state-aided stern-faced automatons. I was too young then to remember that, but from 1953 onwards when I really got interested in athletics Emil quickly became a legend for us. The smiling photographs in the press and the newsreel film of him racing, often chatting with his opponents on the way, and then cheerfully responding to questions afterwards in any one of several languages created a totally different image in our minds to the political ranting about "reds under the bed".

'Gordon Pirie – the rebel hero of every teenage runner then – was copying Emil's training and so was every other distance runner in Britain, and we had dozens of them in World class or very near to it. So we felt we owed a debt to Emil. Then when we heard that he was coming to London in 1955 for the London-v-Prague match we were agog, and that October night at the old White City Stadium he ran against Pirie and Ken Norris at 10,000 metres. To be *truthful, Emil was past his best by then and was well beaten, but I still vividly recall the crowd spending most of the race shouting "Zat-o-pek ! Zat-o-pek ! Zat-o-pek !" rather than "Pi-ree ! Pi-ree ! Pi-ree !". And I think most of us were really rather sorry that Emil lost.*

'If ever I'm asked 'who's the greatest distance-runner ever?'- and it happens quite often – I reply that there was Paavo Nurmi, the great Flying Finn of the 1920s. Then there was Zátopek in the 1940s and 1950s and the prolific Ron Clarke in the 1960s. Then there was also a whole host of Africans – Bikila Abebe, Kip Keino, Haile Gebrselassie, Kenenisa Bekele most obviously. But for me Emil is still the No.1. He revolutionised training methods. No one before him had run anywhere near as hard as he did. Now every distance runner with any pretensions to World-class does. Emil, to me, is up there with Orson Welles, Miles Davis, Edward Hopper – one of the great innovators, and there are not many of them.'

That is the view from abroad, because internationally and particularly to runners of Bob's generation and mine, Zátopek is an enduring memory, and so esteemed that another colleague, Roger Robinson, international cross country runner and professor of English Literature among others things has taken to referring to him in correspondence as 'St Emil'. For a brief period in the years immediately before his death, the Czech media and establishment also came to terms with Zátopek's legacy in more ways than one. In 1997, he was named *Czech Athlete of the Century*, and *Czech Olympian of the Century*. And the final, well-merited accolade came the following year, when President Havel presented him with the Czech Republic's highest honour, the *Order of the White Lion*. But after the grand funeral just before the end of the century, memories began to fade again.

And it is only now that the Czechs are in the process of rediscovering Zátopek. As Prague Marathon race director, Carlo Capalbo had told me, to many people, the younger generation in particular, the once national hero had, due largely to his internal exile, become a forgotten man, and only someone like journalist Štěpán Škorpil was keeping the flame alive. But, not before time, that flicker has burst across the spectrum. When I was running around Stromovka in the summer of 2014, I came across a group of runners with race numbers. I discovered from the next day's newspapers that this was the final event of *Zátopek's Golden Week*. The brainchild of Vlastimil Šroubek, secretary of Plzeň marathon club, Zátopek's three Olympic golds in Helsinki are celebrated with a series of races, run in the same order, on the same date and time of day as he ran them in 1952 – the 10,000 metres on July 20 at 17.45, the 5000 metres on July 24 at 17.50, and the marathon on July 27 at 15.30.

Zátopek's Golden Week races were inaugurated in 2008 in Plzeň, the home base of the organisers but in tandem with the London Olympics the races were moved to Prague in 2012, with the track events in the stadium of Slavia Prague. Šroubek wrote to me, to say, 'The idea to organize this series first occurred to me in autumn 2007. Emil Zátopek is and always has been my idol, because he could manage something what nobody else could ever do. The main goal is to remind the young generation that Emil Zátopek won gold on precisely those days and at those times; and to remind that we had the best long-distance runner of all-time on this planet, who had a strong will, tremendous endurance, to win in just one week (eight days), three Olympic gold medals, and every time an Olympic record, which no one will ever do anymore. This success was also enhanced by the victory of Mrs. Dana Zátopková, which was also a new Olympic record, immediately after the victory of Emil Zátopek in running the 5,000m. Husband and wife Zátopek thus became the most successful married couple of Olympic Games. This series is also organized thanks to Mrs Dana Zátopková. I strongly believe that the series will continue in the coming years and will grow, with the hope that one day maybe there will appear a 'new Emil Zátopek'.

The chances of that happening anytime soon are not high. Zátopek emerged from a society with no tradition whatsoever of long distance running. And when he retired, the situation more or less returned to normal. Of course, the Czech records for his events have improved in the 50 odd years since he retired, although the track record for the rarely run 25,000 metres is still his. But mulling over his races and records one evening, I wondered how they compared with the current bests in Czecho and Slovakia. The sorry story I uncovered was that in his classic distances, 5000 and 10,000 metres, the fastest men in 2015 were, respectively, eighteen seconds and one minute sixteen seconds slower than the Zátopek of 1954! However, *Zátopek's Golden Week* has been steadily growing, with more sponsors coming on board, and will doubtless profit further from the biopic on Zátopek announced at the 50th anniversary of the Karlový Vary film festival in 2015, and by the publication of Pavel Kosatík's *Emil – Běžec* (Emil - Runner) later that year; further, a graphic novel entitled simply *Zátopek*, by Jan Novák and Jaromír Svejdík was published in spring 2016. That was followed by the publication of three books by British writers, including this one; and Dana's sequel to their 1960 autobiography is also due to be published prior to the Rio Olympic Games. The Czech Olympic Committee added a novel way to give impetus to the Zátopek legend. Emil would occasionally append a line-drawing self-portrait to his autograph, an individual version of the one with Dana chasing him with a javelin which you can find on the fly-leaf of this book. The Olympic Committee incorporated his solo cartoon onto their logo for the Rio Olympic kit.

61.

Zátopek's upper body contortions when racing, once memorably described as like, 'wrestling with an octopus,' caused much hilarity, especially in the early days of his career. But looking closely at old film of his running form during races when he is under pressure, mostly chasing others, his gesticulations, facial contortions and eye-rolling, far from being funny, verge on the epileptic. There is no evidence that Zátopek suffered from the condition and, anyway, medical opinion on exercise-induced epilepsy is divided. Maybe it was simply a manifestation of his hyper-activity. You'll remember that I quoted Dana earlier, saying he was more difficult to monitor than a bag of fleas. Because when I suggested to a few of my interviewees that there seemed to be a manic quality about Zátopek, they all agreed immediately. "Yes, absolutely," said historian Pavel Kosatík. "People thought they could run like Zátopek. I think it's impossible. No one could do it his way. And it's good to know it preventively(sic). It was obsessive".

"Exactly, this is a good way to describe it," said his old friend Lada Kořán, who went on to say that even when he was slowing down later in life, often sitting pensively at gatherings of family and friends, and barely taking part in the proceedings, Emil would spring to life at the slightest encouragement. "Dana would say, Emil, tell that story! And he was on his feet immediately, telling the whole story. And then he sat down and relaxed again; but that was already in the final years". Though he never met Zátopek, Ambassador Žantovský had the advantage of having done a psychology degree at Charles University. "I often heard him speaking on the radio.... I so much remember the voice. He spoke like he was in a race, five hundred words a minute. And you had a sense that he spoke faster than he thought. So there was this manic quality, and it's quite possible there may have been a cyclical aspect to his personality. I think the suspicion was that he was a little crazy. He was impulsive, his instincts were in the right place, always, and he always first did the right thing, and then, when he was under pressure, and also probably to save his career, first in athletics, then in coaching, etc, etc, he made compromises and recantations. But the first instinct was always right".

Journalist and family 'minder,' Štěpán Škorpil offered a couple of examples with a slightly different perspective from the many times he had taken Zátopek (and Dana) to give talks in schools, union halls and sports clubs. "With Dana I would prepare five, six questions. After fifteen minutes of Emil talking, I catch microphone and say, sorry Emil, I have question now for Dana, and after two, three minutes, Emil was crazy, saying I haven't spoken for two minutes. He was hyper.... I remember once in the north of Czech Republic. It was a meeting of five or six schools, 600 boys and girls. There were three of us, me as commentator/speaker, Antonín Panenka, it was in September 1976, after the Czechoslovak national team won the European Championship in football, and Antonín Panenka was the penalty kick hero, like Zatopek was the hero in 1952. In the final, 2-2 against Germany, Panenka took the last penalty kick, and you remember maybe, the ball was very slow, and (German goalie, Sepp) Mayer was in the left side, and the ball on the right.

"So in this hall with 600 people, I say, ladies and gentlemen, eighteen-time world record holder, seven-time European and Olympic winner, three times world sportsman of the year, Emil Zátopek, and the crowd, 'Oh,' and little applause; and Antonín Panenka, striker of the penalty kick of the final, and, oh, absolutely fantastic reaction. BUT, after two and half hours of discussion, Antonín Panenka (simulates loud applause), and Emil Zátopek (simulates thunderous applause), it was an eruption, like Santorini. Because when Emil was talking, it wasn't just a smile, and saying I did this and that. But it was (here he simulates Emil dodging back and forth across the stage). It was this and that, and it was not normal. He was a big actor, absolutely super energy". As a corollary to that, Škorpil said that even at the Zátopek home where he was a regular visitor, Emil could not sit still for a moment. "Even when he was 65, 70 years old, he'd be running around the kitchen; he couldn't stay in one place. Sorry, Štěpá, he'd say, I must go and find this for you. And for Dana, Ovečka (my lamb), I'm making something new for the kitchen. He was...." (And here, Škorpil went to the shelf behind his desk, and took down a Czech-English dictionary)... "He was like quicksilver".

The 'cyclical aspect to his personality,' remarked on by Žantovský is also reflected in some of the secret police reports. One of my translators, Esther

Jones-Russell did a good trawl of the StB files and, in addition to the most important reports which I've already quoted she sent me her overview of the rest. 'What I noticed the most is an odd combination of Zátopek claiming to not get involved with politics and then him fairly openly criticising the regime. The police seem to be aware of this pretty early on. For instance in a report dated 26th November 1949, Zátopek is criticised for his attitude towards the Communist regime. The report notes how during a visit to Bucharest, Zátopek responded to a journalist enquiring about the role of sport within Czechoslovakia by saying that he is an athlete and doesn't want anything to do with politics.

Yet, at other times, Zátopek has been quoted saying that if he doesn't join the Communist Party he'll be kicked out of the army, that he has seen political prisoners chained up while working, and that these prisoners are innocent people. According to this report, *'Zátopek mostly ends such interviews by saying "I'll stop talking now, else they'll lock me up".'* This particular report goes on to try to explain Zátopek's *'unfavourable attitude,'* attributing it both to Dana's influence and to his lack of political consciousness which is the result of having attended the Bata school and then focussing so heavily on sport. The report also blames the *'clearly superficial political education'* taking place at the military unit Zátopek's stationed in. The report concludes by recommending that *'Captain Zátopek is sent to a long-term residential political school'.'*

62.

Zátopek had always liked a drink; on his own admission of the numerous times he stops for a pint in *As Told by Dana and Emil*; on the testimony of Roudný who complained that, despite his friend being a Moravian, "He drank wine as if it were beer. I used to say to him, you need to taste it"; and from his Yugoslav rival Mihalić, who said that Zátopek was mystified that he could be teetotal, and tried to convince him he needed a beer now and again. Whether it was from some act of self-conciousness, whether the censors made him put it in, or, more likely he is referring to hard liquor, but there is a passage in the co-autobiography, 'Alcohol is harmful. Personally, I only have a glass now and then, *when it is absolutely necessary* (my italics)'.

However, it seemed to be an open secret that Emil took seriously to drinking to assuage the boredom of his life in exile, evenings spent sequestered in stinking caravans with lumpen colleagues and occasionally with bosses determined to humiliate him. Dana told me, "One man made him carry 50 kilos of cement, and Emil was not strong, he was a runner. But the boss still said, go and carry this cement. But 50 kilos was too much for him (he was close to 50 years old at this time), and the boss said, what are you now, world record holder? The boss was a very simple man, and wanted to feel important. Emil told him to be a world record holder at 10,000 metres, you need to be very thin and very fast; you don't need to carry 50 kilos of cement".

The journalist Štěpán Škorpil echoed Lada Kořán's assessment of the inevitability of Zátopek's resort to alcohol while labouring, especially for someone who liked a drink in the first place. "You know," said Škorpil, "when you are working hard, far from home, away from your wife, and for food, you only have a little meat and pickles, it's easy to drink. In the Czech Republic, the first resort is beer, the second resort is wine. But Jáchymov is not a place for good wine, so after two, three beers, you are going on the rum. It's a typical Czech thing". Whatever the case, the drinking continued when he returned to Prague in the mid-70s. As I said at the beginning, I'd been surprised on arriving at their home at 9.30 in the morning to be offered a beer. When I spent more time in Czecho from 2014 onwards, I discovered that it was not unusual to be offered a beer at any time of day. It is, after all, as Dana says the national beverage. But when I mentioned the early morning offer to my pal Kenth Andersson, who knew Emil better, and was also in Prague for the marathon in 1998, he said pointedly, "Unfortunately, that would not have been Emil's first of the day. I gather he starts drinking the minute he gets up".

For an obsessive personality, it must have been difficult if not impossible to forego the drink once it took hold. Škorpil attracted Dana's ire when he signally failed to stop Emil arriving home blotto after an evening talk in Teplice, just over an hour's drive north of Prague. It was the early 1980s. "After two hours, Emil said, I need a drink," Škorpil told me. "I say to Emil, Dana told me you have to go straight home, she needs you to do something for her. From Teplice to Prague, it is 90k, not a long way, and we return, and on the way is a hill called Pashka Pole. It was a place in the 19th century, there were two highwaymen named Pashka and Pole. And we were going slowly up this hill, and Emil said, 'I really must have something to drink'. At the first village down the hill, about forty five minutes from Teplice, I said, OK, just one beer for you and coca cola for me. But when we went into the road cafe, the clients called out, Zátopek, Škorpil. It was a sports team, and within minutes, I'd lost Emil.

"A few people starting asking me, what do think of this team and that team's chances; and with Emil, it was one glass of whisky, one of vodka, one of rum, one of gin. After a half hour, I said, Emil, Dana will kill me. No, no, no, he said. But, you know, if you take just one type of drink, wine, whisky, cognac, no problem, but everybody wanted to buy Emil something different. I had four cocas, and I'm driving to Troja, and I stopped in front of the house. I said, Emil, are you OK (simulates a drunk response), and he said, please, let Dana be asleep, please. I don't know how long it took him to get from the garden gate to the house; it was only ten metres but slightly uphill. I phoned him after three days, and asked how he got in. 'Štěpá, I don't know'. But that first morning, he said Dana was very angry with him. I didn't hear from Dana for one month. And when I finally went to their house, I said, 'Dana, I'm so sorry,' She said, 'Next time, I'll really kill you,' because the mix of alcohol had made him really ill and miserable." According to Kořán, who saw him shortly before he died, the era of non-alcoholic beer in the late 1990s did not endure. "When he was in hospital, he was absolutely disgusted with his shape; he didn't want to live anymore. He lost interest in fighting. He was going to die, because he didn't want to live. This is the worst you can get. So I bought a few bottles of beer, the one he liked, *Staropramen*. I had a big coat on, and put it in my inside pockets. We came to the room, Dana and I, and I showed him the bottles, and his eyes lit up. He was happy I'd thought about it. We had a last beer".

***

There was a terrible irony in Kořán's demise. He survived almost 20 years in Jáchymov – something he put down to his fine physical fitness – but when he finally let himself be persuaded to write the story of his incarceration, it tangentially contributed to his death. He was making his way to the book launch, not far from where we had met at the Slavia Café in central Prague a few months earlier, when he slipped on a pavement, fell and hit his head. He was taken to hospital immediately, but lay, concussed in intensive care for days. According to his wife and friends, he was transferred far too quickly - before his condition was stabilised – to the local hospital near his Czech home, some 100k south of Prague. He went in and out of consciousness for weeks, and seemed to be making an improvement, when his condition nose-dived in late summer, 2015. He died on September 19th, the birthday of the man he had described to me as, "A fantastic man, and a fantastic friend" - Emil Zátopek.

63.

Emil Zátopek died on November 22, 2000, two months after his 78th birthday. He had had a stroke a month earlier, and was being treated in Prague's military hospital. The former Olympic wrestler, Karel Engel, who was a neighbour of the Zátopeks in the Prague suburb of Troja, telephoned journalist Štěpán Škorpil to tell him the news. Škorpil had become a sort of unpaid guardian to Dana and Emil, and often ferried them around, when they gave talks to schools and sports societies. "Karel called and asked me to make a speech at the funeral, in the traditional burying place in Prague, at Strašnice," Škorpil told me. "It's a very cold place, every funeral is there. I said, no, Karel, the Czech athletic federation and all the world knows Emil, it is impossible for him to go to there. Maybe the stadium of Strahov (scene of many Zátopek successes), where Mimoun was running with Emil 10 kilometres before the Olympic Games in Melbourne; or the National Theatre. That's the place for the funeral for the number one man in Czech sports history.

"Karel said, you know this is impossible, because it is only for poets and actors, and top people. But I remembered that the son of Zdeněk Srstka (Olympic weight-lifter, Rome 1960), his son was director of the National Theatre. So I got on the phone to Srstka's son, and he said, yes, Emil Zátopek, will have his last appearance at the National Theatre, with its atmosphere of history. It was built in 1882, a beautiful place. Juan-Antonio Samaranch (head of the International Olympic Committee) was there, the President of the Czech Republic was there, the president of IAAF (international athletics federation), the Premier of the Government of Czech Republic. There were 800 guests from all over the world, Alain Mimoun for example, I don't know if Herbert Schade was there, but it was very, very interesting.

"That evening, I was with a friend, who lived about 20 kilometres from Prague. He had a new satellite for TV, 260 channels. He called me, and said, come and look with me at the programmes from around the whole world. So we did - click, click, click - and we clicked on *Al Jazeera*, and I said, stop! At that moment, there was a picture from the National Theatre, and Emil Zatopek's funeral. *Al Jazeera* had a one and half minute report. And so did many others, from all around the world".

64.

When I met him almost thirty years after his exile, Emil was philosophical about his change of fortunes, saying, "For sportsmen, it's not bad to do manual work, you need to change to avoid stagnation". But for a man who so enjoyed the limelight, being deprived of the variety of company he kept in Prague and abroad must have compounded the mental if not physical torture that his exile was intended to achieve. I would venture that a man who thrived on personal contact – and I don't think the adulation meant that much – must have been dying slowly from lack of contact with the normal, serious, frivolous world, and being exiled was a shrivelling process for him. When he did return to Prague, apart from the occasional brief TV interviews that Škorpil talked about, and the talks at schools and sports clubs, he was still shunned by the regime, and kept hidden away in the sports archives. He had a brief efflorescence following the Velvet Revolution, when he was restored to national life, and I witnessed him being presented to the crowd at the Olympic Games in Barcelona 1992 and, a nice touch this, handing out the medals for the 5000 metres at the European Championships in Helsinki 1994, a reminder of his finest Olympic victory in the same stadium 42 years earlier. By then he had begun his steady decline; and that would be exacerbated by a collapse during a trip to Athens the following year, 1995.

Dana may have been upset at what she saw as 'mistakes' in Jean Echenoz's re-imagining of Zátopek's life and career, but I was struck by the French writer's evaluation of Zátopek in an interview he gave to *L'Équipe* just before publication of *Courir* in 2008. Echenoz said that he had spent long hours studying in the newspaper archives from the mid-forties to the mid-fifties in the *Bibliothèque Nationale* in Paris. 'During the course of my research, I was truly won over by the disconcerting humility of the character. An artisan, in the noblest sense of the term, who was, I think perfectly honest, a custodian of a kind of life-view, a morality that I imagine a thousand leagues distant from that of his successors". And that, with a dash of French hyperbole is exactly what Ron Clarke said of Zátopek.

The Russians and the regime in Prague may have achieved their objective of shutting him up and driving him to drink. And his recantation of support for the liberalising movement in the late sixties may have tarnished his reputation, especially with the younger generation in the Czech Republic. But no one who ever met Emil Zátopek could forget what a gentle, benign, positive and supportive character he was. And no one who saw him run, even on film and video could forget the ebullience and joy and excellence that he brought to athletics and to the post-war public wherever he went. And to the Czechoslovak people of his own generation, who endured sixty years of Occupation and privation he was a totem of defiance in the face of totalitarianism.

In a century of huge changes, the Second World War was one of the seminal turning points, redrawing boundaries, forging new allegiances, willed or not. Immediately after the War, in his chosen field, Zátopek himself provided one of those turning points. Quite simply, he single-handedly re-invented running; real running, that is, elite competitive running – the pursuit of excellence. Zatopek emerged from an unlikely source at a time of huge social and political change. Czechoslovakia had little or no tradition in distance running. But by dint of personality and will, experiment and evaluation, this country boy introduced a revolution, one which continues to this day. He redefined notions of training which, while recognising his own overindulgence, provided a template which endures. And he had the courage to go to the front and invite opposition; to run from the front and provide an opportunity to be beaten. He put himself on the line in the pursuit of excellence. As the results indicate, the vast majority of the time he succeeded. Four Olympic titles, three European golds, eighteen world records, and six years unbeaten in his speciality is only statistical proof of his superiority, a domination that he forged through the will to endure lonely hours and days, weeks and years of effort on the training track. No man more deserved his success and his kudos.

Emil Zátopek was a one-off, perhaps the most singular character in the history of track and field athletics, which has had more than its fair share of eccentrics. That he was deeply loved is clear from the testimonials recounted here. That in part was due to his generosity which seemed boundless. Giving away an Olympic gold medal (and other baubles) is abundant proof of his philosophy that it is the performance not the prize which counts. And there is no better testimony for a man who stood and ran astride his century. And not just his own century. When he visited the stadium in Olympia, and paid his respects to the Ancient Hellenic athletes whose feats date back four thousand years, he will have recognised that his own place in the pantheon is secure.

Emil Zátopek is one of the immortals.

Acknowledgements

My thanks to Dana Zátopková for her memories and accessibility, and for permission to use personal photographs. Thanks equally to Carlo Capalbo for his enormous help, and to all his staff at RunCzech/Prague International Marathon, particularly Diana Rybachenko and Jarmila Krauskopfová; to my driver/interpreter Bojan Nanković, and to Zdenka Pecková, Zhanna Agakashieva and Dario Monti for helping to organise my programme; to Davor Savija for keeping the faith after Zane Branson's untimely death; and to my training partners, Slavo Michalík, Evgeniya Zhgir and Sašo Belovski.

On the home front, I am grateful to family and friends, Peggy Paterson, Kevin Grogan and James O'Brien for proofing, editing, pre-publication reading and advice on photographs; to Renata Clark at the Czech Centre, London, and to Norman Giller for his advice on the pitfalls of self-publishing; and especially to Peter Nichols for his advice and expertise with lay-out and design.

Thanks to my translators, Esther Jones-Russell, Kate Lustigová, Rebecca Seaton, and Tomás Kubát; and also to Dana's neighbour/guardian Karel Engel; and not least to the numerous interviewees and drinking companions who made my extended stays in Prague and elsewhere in the Czech Republic so memorable.

London, July 2016

197

INDEX